ADVANCE PRAISE FOR
SOUL WARRIOR

*How to Liberate Yourself from Survival Mode
and Thrive Through Any Challenge*

"Soul Warrior is so rich, so true, and so well-written. The lessons and lightbulb moments literally knocked me back. Angela demonstrates the importance of taking responsibility for your own words and actions, alongside the importance of being kind, to others and to yourself, while learning a new way to live. It's not easy, but Angela's guidance and perspective gives me the courage to just do it. I love what she does. It's a gift."

— Dawn Russell,
CEO of Treats for Chickens

"The world needs more teachers like Angela to guide those who are ready to do the work, wake-up to themselves, and transform their turmoil into potential."

— Dr. Nicole LePera,
NY Times Best-Selling
Author of *How To Do The Work*

"Brilliant and succinct! It made me pause many times. The world needs Angela's wisdom. We all need to be heard, and Angela will hear you and your need to feel safe."

— Win Normandi,
Watercolor Artist & Angela's Mother

"Angela's book, and her accurate depiction of what it means to be a human on this planet, struck a multitude of chords within my soul, captivating something inside of me that yearns to be discovered. The part of me that strives to grow was activated by the story of her existence. I am grateful Angela put it into words, not just for me, but for anyone to read, because Soul Warrior is universally impactful."

— Emily Cox Turek,
Holistic Practitioner

"When I first met Angela, I was grief-stricken, self-loathing, and lost, but her guidance brought me to understand my true nature, igniting my inner light and introducing me to my voice. Now, ten years later, after working together to complete her masterpiece – a book bound by the power of reflection, compassion, and transformation – it became clear to me how eternally relevant the practice of Soul Work is to maintaining that light and pursuing my purpose. I guarantee everyone who reads this book will be affected by it."

— Sophia Claringbull,
Consulting Editor for Soul Warrior

"Why are we like this and how can we get back to ourselves to live our lives in truth? Angela's life story and how she came to this place of being and work makes the journey a tangible and relatable resting place. Soul Work, through all the visceral responses, is as close to myself as I've ever allowed."

— Laura Fraize,
Event Planner, Mother, and
Transformational Soul Work Client

"Soul Warrior, and Angela's vulnerable and powerful storytelling, offers intense and raw insight into the journey of life – from fierce motherhood to familial trauma, love, loss, healing, and survival – and it serves as an invitation for others to do the same."

— Krista Ripma,
Marketing Expert, Business Coach &
Founder of Authentic Audience

"Angela compassionately guides us through difficult life circumstances and deep inner work to finally reveal the light of our true selves. I found parallels to my own healing journey with cancer. The sacred practices of Transformational Soul Work lead us towards self-love and authenticity, enabling us to step into conscious wellness by weaving mind, body and spirit in alignment with our full vitality."

— Katharine Shotz,
Marriage Family Therapist

"An honest, relatable, and thought-provoking story that ignites self-inquiry and inspires the reader to make a conscious choice to be themselves. From the testament of her own transformation, Angela's practice has the potential to change your life."

— Jennifer Grais,
Shamanic Healer, Singer, Author of
Christa's Luck

Disclaimer

"This work is used for the purpose of self discovery, self improvement, and self empowerment. I make no claim that these services will replace your existing health and well being regime."

Karen -
Here's to Thriving
in Life

Love Angela

Soul
Warrior

*How to Liberate Yourself from
Survival Mode and Thrive Through
Any Challenge*

ANGELA DESALVO

Deep
Pacific
Press

Soul Warrior

How to Liberate Yourself from Survival

Mode and Thrive Through Any Challenge

Angela DeSalvo

Copyright © 2022 Angela DeSalvo

Deep
Pacific
Press

Deep Pacific Press
117 E 37th Street #580
Loveland, CO 80538
http://DeepPacificPress.com

Cover Design by Quantum Shift Media
Cover Image ©Agsandrew via Canva.com

ISBN 978-1-956108-02-6 (paperback)
ISBN 978-1-956108-03-3 (eBook)

angela@angeladesalvo.net
www.angeladesalvo.net

DEDICATION

When my girls look back on their childhood, I hope they see I was someone who tried to instill in them the desire to be conscious and present, to follow their truth, and to be okay with who they are. I wish for them to realize that we do the best we can at any given moment, and there is always room for growth and improvement.

I hope they can look back and take with them a lesson of compassion, and know that for every struggle they personally encounter, someone else is struggling as well. I hope kindness is at the forefront for them when it comes to dealing with other people.

My hope for my girls is that they know my role as their mother was entered into with full intention and desire to love them as deeply as possible. I tried, and will forever try, to do my best in every moment to raise them as strong, independent, confident young women who will continue to search for what is important to them, doing so from a place of love, compassion, passion, and a willingness to be all they are meant to be.

I love you both beyond measure.

Your grateful mother.

CONTENTS

ACKNOWLEDGEMENTS

I consider the work expressed in this book just as important as giving birth to and raising my two daughters, as though *I* were my own third child, whom I raised through years of self-inquiry, writing, and Soul Work.

I would like to acknowledge the following people for nurturing my growth and supporting me while I wrote this book. Thank you Alanna and Maria, my daughters, and my pride and joy. The life we share together has been the fertile ground from which I am able to reparent myself.

I thank my mother and father, Win and Jim Normandi, for bringing me into this world and providing a constant source of love, despite the inevitable transference of generational pain. My older brothers, Tony and Jim, who while they may not have realized it, offered me a place to be myself when I was younger.

Ellen Fishburn, because without her business, Giving Spirit Form, I may have never discovered the deep, dark places within myself I had no idea I was hiding from, and therefore, may have never written this book. Emily Cox Turek, for introducing me to Ellen, but mostly for being a beacon of light in my life and arriving when I, the student, was ready to be seen.

My exceptionally talented and gifted editor, Sophia Claringbull, without whose help I would not have been able to complete my manuscript. Boundless appreciation is not enough to express what she has helped me do to realize a lifetime of desire to write this book.

I want to acknowledge the friends who took the time to read my book while it was still a work in progress. They reflected back to me that my human experience is relatable, and that a deeper sense of self-awareness is always around the corner, if and when a person is ready.

And with my deepest gratitude, I wish to thank my husband, Doug. It is with great regard, respect, and admiration for the man, father, and husband that he is, that my choice to explore the unknowns of myself has made us richer in our partnership with a foundation of togetherness.

And lastly, the powers that be that are greater than us all, allowing for clarity and understanding to manifest in human form so we may experience a life of abundance, joy, and gratitude.

INTRODUCTION

Many of us live within the subconscious constraints of our minds, day after day replaying the same stories of who we think we are. There is great comfort in this pattern of familiar behavior, but it can also keep us closed off from the present moment, unavailable to opportunity, and unaware of our potential.

The story of my life – from the *core wounds* of my childhood and the trauma, implicit beliefs, and conditioned behaviors that resulted, through crises and codependency, and into the reclamation of my voice and the rebirth of my authentic self – will likely shed some insight into your own. The human experience shares many similarities, and yet, we can often feel so alone.

My hope is that you will find just a grain of resonance in my experiences that ignites your desire to embrace your own full expression of self, and to become aware of the conditioned behaviors that cause you to react from your past and prevent you from responding in the present. My desire is for you to experience a version of yourself that you are proud of. Being the true *you* is the best gift you can give yourself in this lifetime, and it's one I continue to unwrap.

Soul Work is a method of practicing self-inquiry I developed through years of educating myself on my true self. It is a never-ending journey that holds the key to freely expressing yourself. Hopefully, by revealing the details behind how I discovered the benefits of Soul Work for myself, you'll begin to see some common threads in your own life and be inspired to understand the truth of who you are. Ideally, you'll finish reading this book with the desire to live fully expressed and consciously aware, rather than piloted by conditioned behavior.

This book begins as a memoir in Part One, and culminates as a teaching of Soul Work in Part Two. It consists of the reflections I required in order to become aware of my true self, along with the elements of Soul Work I practice and guide others in to feel safe and continue to heal. This is foundational to how I operate, and has allowed me to be in the mystery of life while also trusting in the unknown, something that used to utterly stop me in my tracks. Doubt, fear or insecurity may sneak in from time to time, but nowhere to the degree they used to.

When I trust in the unknown, I am able to access the grace and gratitude of being a spiritual being who is having a human experience. This allows me to come back to myself over and over again, regardless of how hard life is. And it is hard! There is life force energy in the acceptance of hardships, and I've witnessed plenty in my life, as you'll learn in the coming chapters.

As you read this book, I challenge you to become a witness to your own narrative of how you show up in life, and thus, begin to connect the dots of what it means for you to know thyself, feel safe in the world, and experience the joy of making your own conscious choices. This is the transformative goal behind Soul Work, and the reason why I connect with others to guide them in their own journeys towards healing and liberation. The process will not always be comfortable, but I promise you, it is worthwhile.

If and when, while reading this book, you become triggered by your own memories and experiences, I encourage you to be kind to yourself, take breaks, and utilize the Journal included in Part Three of this book to help you navigate emotions that arise as you begin your own Soul Work journey. I invite you to consider what you need to remember, accept, face, witness, acknowledge, embrace, discover, practice, reconnect with, rejoice in, and offer to others in order to feel whole, true, and free.

PART 1

AN INTIMATE PERSPECTIVE

"If your mind is empty, it is always ready for anything, it is open to everything. In the beginner's mind there are many possibilities, but in the expert's mind there are few."

Shunryu Suzuki, Zen Mind, Beginner's Mind:
Informal Talks on Zen Meditation and Practice

CHAPTER 1

REMEMBER: THE CALLING

"Each person enters the world *called*, like an oak tree,
to fulfill their soul's agenda."

James Hillman,
*The Soul's Code: In Search of Character
and Calling*

"What do you want me to say?" I asked, and then I heard her voice.

At first, I didn't write anything.
I was frozen in my fascination,
until she said, "WRITE THIS!"
My pen took it from there.

Melissa had hoped to make it to her thirty-fifth birthday, but she was three months shy of getting there. We were high school friends who'd lost contact after our college years. When I discovered Melissa had been given a cancer diagnosis, I knew I needed to be in her life again. Melissa had a rare cancer, found during a routine eye check that showed a tumor behind her eye. Her only symptoms had been a "cold" that wouldn't go away.

I had the pleasure of spending one day a week with her for the last year of her life. Thursday was my day. I'd drop my kids at school (they were three and six years old at the time), and make the forty-five minute drive across the Richmond bridge to her home in Oakland. I'd spend six to eight hours with her, visiting, making her food, and taking her to appointments. Whatever the time called for, I was a support in any way I needed to be for her during this time.

Melissa's house was very warm and inviting with its rich mahogany wood trim. The kitchen was cute and cozy. It felt like our family ranch in Petaluma with its 40's style feel. Antiquated but functional, the homey kitchen was made for sitting at the table and discussing life as a natural occurrence, which Melissa and I did often. Those Thursdays were especially sacred because of this. While our lives had gone in different directions over the ten years prior, we were now reunited, and I looked forward to this quality time. It lasted for one year – that's how long she survived the cancer. During our time together, I said to her that if she knew what I was supposed to do in my life for her to tell me when she got to the other side.

It was February 1999. I'd decided to lay down for a nap. My daughters had plans and were taken care of after school. It was one of those naps where I was trying to wake up and couldn't. I heard lots of commotion, and in my half-awake half dream state, I thought it was coming from upstairs. I heard the phone ringing, but didn't answer it because I couldn't wake myself up. I heard lots of confusion, panic and crying.

It was as though I was in-between worlds. One in which I was asleep on my bed, and one where a group of people were witnessing Melissa's final breaths and it stirred a bit of a panic among them. Once I finally landed back in my body, I could move again and was able to wake up. I went upstairs and listened to the recording on the machine. Melissa's partner had left me a message – Melissa had just died. Of course, she did. It all made sense now. *I was between worlds.* I was in the ethereal world of her dying and hearing the people present to her, along with their emotional responses. I was hearing it as it was happening, only to wake to actually hearing the confirmation on my recorder.

I went to her house the day after she died. Her partner and friends, who had become her family, had decided along with Melissa to keep her body at home for forty hours. The belief was that was the time needed for her spirit to rise up and out of her body. While I had spent one day a week with her for a year, nothing can prepare you for the death of a loved one. I walked in the room and saw my dear friend – who'd been speaking to me just days before – lying there motionless.

Her skin was a grayish hue, her body cold and rigid to touch. I dropped to my knees. Overcome with tears as I laid my hands on her body, I felt a warmth enveloping me from behind as though I were being embraced by a blanket. It was Melissa – she was comforting me in my sorrow and telling me all was okay.

A few days later she was being cremated, and a group of about ten people, myself included, wanted to sit outside the crematorium. I didn't know those people well at all, only her partner, whom I'd met a few times. I wanted to be there for this ceremony of sorts as we sat outside while her body was burning inside. We sat in a big circle without any clear intention or purpose. It was apparent, as we all sat in silence, that our thoughts were on Melissa.

I was sitting on the curb, and as clear as the day was bright, I saw Melissa appear in front of me, kneel down, and say, "Listen, everyone is pulling for me. I can't go to everyone. You need to gather them all together."

While she was telling me this, a garbage truck was making a ruckus of noise a few blocks down. She looked over my head and said, "Oh geez!" as if to make a fuss over the noise of the truck. She was trying to tell me to gather this group in a circle by holding hands so she could collectively surround us with her energy.

Well, for one, this was not my everyday conversation with the deceased. Secondly, I only knew one of the people in this group, and she was only an acquaintance. Thirdly, I wasn't one to speak up much then. I had made it apparent, however, that I needed to be in her life when a gathering was called to inform those who cared that she was sick. Needless to say, I didn't do anything with the information she wanted me to give to everyone. I wish I had trusted myself. I can only imagine the powerful experience it could have been for all of us. What I did do, however, was read at her funeral like she'd asked me to before she died.

It was a few days since Melissa had passed before I sat down to ponder what I would say. The kids were put to bed, the kitchen was cleaned from dinner, and my husband was working in his office. I sat in a wicker chair in our kitchen, at our glass table, and peered outside into the dark night sky, my hand on my forehead and a pen in my hand. I raised my right hand up and grappled out loud, "What do you want me to say?!" as I dropped the pen from my hand and my palm dropped to the table.

I started to hear Melissa's voice! I could even make out her face in front of me, to the left, out and up. If I was at 6 o'clock, she was at 10 o'clock.

When she commanded me to, "Write this!" I wrote everything she told me to.

～2～

Six weeks earlier, I'd been wiping down the same kitchen table when I felt a physical push knock me off my balance. Right as it happened, I thought of my friend Phill. I took notice of this thought, and I identified the push as odd, but I continued to wipe down the table. I then had a strong urge to sit down with the newspaper and look at the obituaries. I felt called to do this as the desire was not mine alone. I opened the Marin Independent Journal to find Phill listed in the obituaries. He'd died on my husband's birthday, a few days earlier. We'd met at a job in the early '80s at a local gym/rehab center. Turned out we had some mutual friends. Our friendship consisted of deep conversations about the mysteries of life, while also maintaining the practical day-to-day tasks of working together.

It all made sense – the push I experienced as I was cleaning the table, the thought I had of Phill that followed, and then being driven to read the obituaries only to find him there. Phill was informing me of his passing. We hadn't spoken in several years as our lives had gone separate ways, but for the next three weeks I'd have visions of him popping up in my space, whether it was in my bathroom, at a coffee shop or at my brother's house. Phill was with me and talking to me as though he was still alive in this realm. I wasn't scared by these occurrences, rather, I felt them as very real. We would "talk" as we had when he was in his physical body. His death was sudden, and I think he wasn't ready to go. The connection we had while he was alive was deep, which made the connection we had after he died very easy to access.

Fast forward six weeks. I'm sitting at my kitchen table in a strange state of awe, having just written Melissa's message, so I thought I'd try connecting with Phill. In my head, I called out his name and asked if there was anything he wanted to say. I heard his voice and wrote the words I heard from him. They were distinctly different from Melissa's.

At the height of my curiosity by then, I called out to my husband's father, who died when my husband was only two-and-a-half years old – and I heard him speak in his New York accent! The words I wrote that came from him described moments in my husband's life that had happened long after his father had died. I showed my husband the three separate messages, and he said, "These aren't your words!" They weren't. They were the words spoken to me by three people who had died.

It was clear to me Melissa's message was distinctly her own, and I knew what I was supposed to say at her funeral. While speaking to her family and friends, I preceded my talk by telling this story. Her father requested a copy, which I gave him. Aside from that copy, I stuck these three different readings from my evening at the kitchen table in a drawer, and went on focusing on raising my young daughters.

I've had many unexplainable episodes in my life of seemingly illogical occurrences, especially having to do with sensing, hearing or seeing from the beyond. However, it wasn't until a decade later I'd have a label for myself and a better understanding of my natural ability I discovered while sitting at my kitchen table.

The year 1999 started with the loss of my friend and ended with catastrophe. On All Saints Day (November 1st), my oldest brother had a terrible and unfortunate accident with the mental health professionals responsible for his care. Due to a lawsuit that transpired because of this accident, all I can really say is my brother Tony remained in a vegetative state and lived between four different hospitals until his final breath, a little over ten years later. My brother had suffered with mental illness, on and off his medication and in and out of mental facilities, for much of his life.

I was in the ICU with him just a few days after his accident. Tony hadn't opened his eyes yet. Alone with him in the room, I looked over and he opened his eyes! I went over to him, held his hand and told him I loved him. He looked at me and mouthed, "I love you." No sound left his mouth, but I heard him. I will cherish this forever. He went back into his comatose state, and over the next ten years, only showed signs of hearing us at appropriate times, turning his head or blinking when things were said that elicited a response.

Two years into his injury, he was brought to a hospital due to an infection that was beyond the scope of the facility where he was residing. The doctors had done some tests and informed us his kidneys were shutting down and he may not make it through the night. My parents, myself and my sister-in-law were in his room at the time.

I was at his bedside and went to leave. I got to the foot of his bed and suddenly, to me, the room had a deafening silence. I looked at Tony and felt a strong pulling sensation. Imagine a vertical hula hoop. The energy was pulling me back to his bedside. I heeded the call and went to the right side of his bed, placing my left hand on his shoulder and my right hand on his wrist. Over the next several minutes, I saw all these images being thrown out, as though memories he no longer needed were being tossed out of him. They had the flavor of childhood activities. By this time, my sister-in-law was standing behind me, bracing me. The energy between Tony and me was so intense I couldn't take my hands off his body – they felt magnetized to him, as though he was using my life force to activate something deeper in himself.

I didn't understand what was happening, I was just going along with it. I thought he was leaving his body, and yet my mom, with her hand on his heart, said, "His heart is beating fine." This went on for several minutes. By the time the energy ceased I was able to remove my hands. I was utterly exhausted. Feeling like everything had been taken out of me, I laid down on the other bed in the room and fell asleep.

The doctors came in a few hours later. After taking more blood tests from Tony, they were shocked to see his numbers had turned around and his kidneys had begun doing their job again! A few days later, Tony was sent back to the care facility. Tony lived for eight more years, albeit in a vegetative state, but what transpired between us that day, when I agreed to respond to that invisible pull of the hula hoop's energy, offered him more time to remain in this world. Obviously, that is what his soul needed.

Tony passed away in January, 2010. In December, 2012, I went to a medium and Tony came through. His message to me was, "It's right under your nose, Ang." I didn't realize what he meant until I returned home and sat at my computer. Earlier that week, I'd seen an advertisement on something that caught my eye and saved it to view later. Well, later had arrived, and I was watching what I'd found earlier. It was a video of Sue Frederick, an intuitive, speaking on how she could tap into hearing people from beyond and helping those who'd lost loved ones. I sat dumbfounded, and said to myself, "That is what I do." Although, I hadn't really done it since the night I heard Melissa… thirteen years earlier!

Oh my gosh! I finally had the epiphany. Between Tony's message that it was right under my nose, and the fact I'd asked Melissa before she died if she knew what I was supposed to do with my life, I finally realized she did in fact "tell me what to do." I was meant to share my gifts with the world.

I am many things to many people. I am clairaudient, clairsentient, clairvoyant and claircognizant. I hear voices, see images, recognize feelings, and I have a sense of "knowing" something beyond myself. Melissa told me right away what I was supposed to do in this lifetime. It just took me a decade or so to really understand it.

CHAPTER 2

ACCEPT: THE CRISIS

"We cannot change anything until we accept it.
Condemnation does not liberate, it oppresses."

Carl Jung,
Modern Man in Search of a Soul

"Okay, it's all been arranged. You will take your finals early so we can spend the entire week in Florida before the wedding."

I remember the discussion well. In order for us to go on vacation and attend my niece's wedding, I had to work it out with Alanna's freshmen teachers first. All the teachers were on board but one. We were in the kitchen, and Doug said, "I just don't have a good feeling about this. Why don't you just go with your parents?"

When we got the invitation to the wedding, my dad's first thought was that only he and my mom would attend. After all, it was going to be a big expense for everyone, and it was at the end of the school year for our kids (Alanna was in her first year of high school and Maria was in middle school). Nonetheless, my mom wanted us to be one big happy family, and I bought into my mom's idea of togetherness and doing it for the good of the whole. I was drawn into the concept of it all. It could be fun to all be together, and I was in my appeasing mode – make my mom happy.

I remember the look on Alanna's face, like, "Yea, Mom, this all feels like too much." Yet, because of me and my desire for us all to be together and not allow myself the freedom to leave my family, I suggested we just go for the weekend. That seemed reasonable and doable for everyone. No one had to miss school or work. We took the redeye out so Doug could work.

The entire crew failed to show up for our redeye flight, causing a major delay. When we finally got to the hotel the next morning, I was completely exhausted. I stayed in the hotel and slept while Doug took the girls swimming with the rest of the family. The next day, we went to Disney World before the evening wedding. We were debating whether to buy one or two-day tickets. Alanna suggested one-day tickets. "What if something happens?" she said.

Florida in the middle of summer is unbearable. It was 105 degrees at a 6 pm outdoor wedding. We were all dripping wet with sweat. As we were dropped off at the wedding by the driver who'd taken us in a van, I ignored the voice in my head that said, "Tell him to come back at 10 pm to get us." Instead, we just said, "We'll call you when we're ready."

The wedding was lovely. When it ended, we decided to go back to the hotel and go swimming. My brother, Jim, and his family had rented a van, and Carol, my sister-in-law, offered to drive us back first and then come back to get her family. In my appeasing way, I said, "Oh no, you go ahead. We'll get a cab." She offered again and I declined again, ignoring the voice that said, "Just go back now." I didn't want to seem selfish by leaving first. I didn't want to be a burden. She then offered to take the kids with her, and I agreed.

I called the cab as they left. We ended up waiting and waiting – no cab. We called again, and he told us he couldn't find us, so we walked away from the venue, up to the main street and into a restaurant to call another cab. In the meantime, Carol was not picking up her phone, which I later found out was because she'd left it in the room while they went to the pool.

Finally, an hour later, we got picked up for the twenty-something minute drive back to the hotel. It was 11 pm or later at this point. The cab driver offered to drop us off right at the pool, but I suggested we go to the room first to get our suits on.

While we were walking to the pool, I asked Doug, who hadn't been keen on going to Florida in the first place, "Well, now we're here, are you having a good time?"

"Yea, I guess," he said.

We were within about thirty feet of the pool entrance when my cousin ran out toward the club house area. I said, "Wow, she's in a hurry! She must have to go to the bathroom."

She turned and saw us.

"Hurry up, Alanna's been hurt!" she shouted urgently. "She can't move. She's asking for her dad."

It had happened within the five minutes before we arrived at the pool. Had we been dropped off by the cab driver, we would have been there. I would have alerted her to be cautious around the slippery ledge of the shallow end.

Doug immediately ran into the pool area. I was in a slow walk behind him, not knowing what to expect, nor wanting to find out.

My baby girl is in the pool, near the steps, on her back.
She is unable to move or feel her body.

Playing tag with her cousins, she'd slipped and fallen off the wet pool ledge into 3.5 feet of water – breaking her neck and becoming instantly paralyzed. Doug, a chiropractor, knew exactly what had just occurred. I was in total shock and complete denial. Alanna was in shock too, but was very present, calm, and composed.

We waited for paramedics to arrive and get Alanna safely on a stretcher. A helicopter arrived on the scene, ready to airlift Alanna to the closest trauma hospital. I walked over with the paramedics, assuming I could go with her. They told me, because of weight issues, I could not go. We would be escorted to the hospital by police. It was thirty minutes away – the level one trauma hospital in Orlando.

I watched my daughter go into the helicopter while the paramedic alerted me to the possibility her lungs could collapse. I asked for just a moment so I could recite the Prayer of Protection over her. As the helicopter took off, I stood dumbfounded, in shock. It took a moment for Doug, Maria and I to find one another.

We squished into the back seat of a town car for the longest thirty minutes I've ever experienced. My parents and brother drove the rental car to meet us there.

We were dropped at the front entrance and met by a chaplain. My heart sank, and my hand pushed out a hard *NO* towards this man, followed by a stern, "No, no, no," coming out of my mouth. Doug followed right behind me and had more sense, inquiring why he was there. Apparently, this was how they greeted all families coming in!

The three of us were guided to a small, dark waiting room, and my family arrived moments later. We waited in silent, nervous anticipation of what we'd learn of Alanna and her current state. It seemed like an eternity, until finally the doctor came in and took a chair.

> Alanna has a burst fracture of C5.
> She is paralyzed from the chest down.
> I'm in shock.
> I'm not really processing this yet.
> The tone of the room is confused.
> Maria, just eleven years old, screams,
> "What is paralyzed!?"
> "She can't move her body," I say.
> Maria is wailing.
> We are all in disbelief.

Since Alanna had arrived at the hospital, doctors had run MRIs, CAT scans, injected her with prednisone (a common treatment for spinal cord injury), and attached a 20lb halo to her skull to keep the pressure off her damaged spinal cord. They let us into the emergency room (ER) to see Alanna lying flat on a bed with the halo drilled into her skull. She couldn't move anything.

The first thing she said to us was, "It's ok, you guys."

"How do you know that?" I asked.

"Because it can't not be," she replied.

Dr. Gupta, a gentle man, took me over to see the image of my daughter's injured spinal cord on film. All I could say was, "Will this kill her?"

"No," he immediately assured me. "It is an injury to her spinal cord and her body will be affected, but it will not kill her."

The nurses in the department must have had a sixth sense. The next thing I remember was a nurse coming up from behind me to hold me up. She must have seen my knees buckling before I even realized they were.

Shit, shit, shit!! I began going over all the would've, could've, should'ves that could have prevented this from occurring.

Alanna then reassured me, "Mom, this could have happened anywhere. It's not because we came to Florida."

Yes, but as I looked back, there were all the signs I ignored along the way that could have changed the course of things. Telling the cab to come back at 10 pm. Taking the ride Carol offered. Stopping at the pool first before getting my suit. Not going on the trip at all!

Walking to the hospital bathroom with my brother, I exclaimed, "I don't know how to do this!" I didn't know how to take care of my daughter in her current state. All I knew was it was my job to take care of her, and I would learn whatever was necessary to do that.

About ten hours after Alanna's injury, she endured a four-hour surgery to stabilize her neck with a metal plate. I remember the doctor coming to show us pictures and telling us what the surgery meant. He said, "I've cleaned out all the fragments of bone near her spinal cord."

Ok, I thought. *She's going to be alright. Everything is cleaned up! They've fixed her spinal cord.* Boy, was I naive or in deep denial! Her spinal cord had been damaged – paralysis was the result.

Alanna stayed a week in the ICU at Arnold Palmer Children's Hospital in Florida. Doug and I stayed across the street in a home for parents of kids in the hospital. Maria stayed with my brother and his family for a few days while we got settled, then they all went back home to California. My gut feeling was Maria should have stayed with us, but I let my inner voice get overridden, again, by listening to others saying that structure and familiar surroundings would be better for her than staying with us at the hospital. She was able to finish her last week of sixth grade and had a few different families taking care of her.

My parents continued on for the week with us. My family was used to hospitals and crises, we'd had lots of practice with Tony's episodes, and my mom and brother's cancer treatments. We'd always been there for each other in times like these.

After a week, it was time to get back to California, but not home, at least for Alanna and myself. It would be four months before we both went home to sleep in our own beds.

We took a private jet, not the luxurious kind we imagined when we heard of the flight, but a small plane that contained Alanna on a stretcher and necessary IVs, the pilot, a nurse, and Doug and I sitting wherever there was room left over. I remember sitting on a stump that got extremely hot. We had to refuel in Texas on our way to Oakland Children's Hospital.

We were met on a small runway at Oakland by my parents, Maria, and an ambulance that took Alanna to the hospital.

If being at the Florida Hospital was a bad dream, then entering this hospital was like a nightmare. We went from a large, private, quiet room in an ICU to a very loud, very busy Friday night and a crowded, double-occupancy room at Oakland Children's Hospital. I was tired and smelly from the long day of travel, and we were instantly bombarded by doctors and nurses doing their jobs. They were expecting Alanna and had her bed ready in the room we would be sharing with a stranger.

Alanna had not showered since she'd been in the ICU in Florida. Her hair had been in a bun atop her head for a week, still left over from the night in the swimming pool. I went with the nurse as she pushed Alanna on a gurney to go have a shower, which had to be taken on the gurney as Alanna was in no state to hold her body up.

As the hair tie was taken out, big clumps of her hair fell into my hands. The pain and disbelief of what was occurring hit me at every turn, yet I had to be strong for Alanna. I felt I had to endure this pain right alongside her, but in a way that lifted her up, rather than pull her down into despair. I think we were both doing this for each other.

Even though Alanna received a room when we arrived, we still had to undergo the formalities of registering her into the hospital. Maria went downstairs with me, and as the receptionist was taking the personal information she needed, I experienced another blow to my reality as she confirmed with me Alanna's diagnosis of quadriplegia. I abruptly exclaimed, "NO!" I thought, *What the hell is she talking about? That's not my daughter.* Part of me didn't even know what it meant.

"Oh," she said. "Ok." I could tell she realized I was obviously still in shock and complete denial.

Maria, the sweet, wise child she was, said, "It's ok, Mom. It's ok." She also helped us find our way back upstairs to the room, as I was disoriented in the hospital, which was in a state of remodel.

Doug and I, and my dad, had to sit with the head doctor of the floor and listen all over again about Alanna's diagnosis and future prognosis. Dr. Gupta in Florida had given us hope. He told us it could take eighteen months before we saw what Alanna's condition could be. This doctor delivered us little hope as he spewed out statistics on spinal cord injuries. While he may have been a realist, I am an idealist. Listening to his worst-case scenarios about my daughter's future was nothing I wanted to be a part of. His words left me feeling helpless, yet something inside of me demanded to be hopeful. It was the old familiar feeling I'd learned growing up with crises – don't give up, ever. Doug and I weren't going to sit back and accept this man's doom and gloom for our daughter. We both intuitively decided moving forward was the only way to go, and we would do anything and everything in our power to help Alanna heal.

Disenchanted with Oakland Children's Hospital and their end game for Alanna, we went on the hunt for a more aggressive rehab facility that offered a bit more hope for recovery. Oakland was there to try and stabilize Alanna, and to send her home within six weeks, when the insurance deemed her ready to go home. We stayed for only three.

Our time there included the rehabilitation of her ability to project her voice beyond a whisper. Alanna had been on a feeding tube for a couple of weeks before she learned to swallow correctly. She was gaining back some initial use of her arms and learning to feed herself after coming off the feeding tube. She also learned how to eat with a utensil strapped to her hand. It took more than a few goes for her to direct her hand to her mouth. The fact that she could even raise her arm to do this was a blessing, given her level of injury.

Those three weeks were filled with visitors and the search for the perfect sweet potato pie. Alanna had become obsessed with having sweet potato pie as it was soft and tasty. I remember so clearly the day the physical therapist sat Alanna up – the first time she would actually experience her body against gravity. I was standing alone outside her hospital room as they sat her on the edge of her bed. It was as though her body was made of jelly. Alanna said, "Whoa," as she was unable to control any part of her body. I sat there in disbelief. What was my daughter going to be up against with this new life of hers? Of ours?

I was giving updates on Alanna's progress through a website a friend had set up for her. Any new movement was documented and celebrated. Doug and I split the nights at the hospital until it became too hard for him to work after a night's sleep there. Maria spent those days at dance camp and with various friends and family members.

After those three weeks, we decided to move on to Shriner's Children's Hospital in Sacramento. Dr. Dread from Oakland (as we referred to him, and I've since forgotten his name) told us, "Why bother? Nothing is going to change Alanna's outcome." I was so disgusted with that man, and recall telling him I had no interest in what he had to say. While that was his opinion, we were moving forward in hope. (I was at home, packing my bags for a three-month stay at Shriner's when I had that conversation with him.)

Juggling these decisions around Alanna's immediate care also coincided with Maria's twelfth birthday. Fortunately, prior to our trip to Florida, I had already signed Maria up for a sleep-away tennis camp located only an hour and a half away from Shriner's, allowing Maria to still celebrate with friends and making it easier for Doug and I to pick her up. Alanna's scheduled sleep-away volleyball camp, obviously, had to be cancelled.

I drove to Shriner's behind the ambulance that took Alanna there. We were greeted by a wonderful, kind female nurse, Lari. She eased us into our stay, making everything very accommodating. Were it not for the injury, it almost felt like we were at a nice hotel. That feeling wore off after a few hours, when all I could think was *oh my god, is this as good as it's going to get for Alanna?* She had very little functional control of her body and was assigned to a wheelchair, and yet she'd spent most of her time in bed at Oakland.

So, there we were, Alanna and I beginning to navigate this whole new life together. Doug and Maria came up every weekend and stayed at the hotel across the street, giving me a chance to spend a night uninterrupted by nurses. We even threw a belated birthday party for Maria at Shriner's so her sister could be present. Life was limited, especially then, as we learned of Alanna's physical capacities on a daily basis. I dropped about twelve pounds from the stress.

For four years, I gave myself away, because that's what I knew how to do. Give without regret. Give because it's the right thing to do. Give because I could, and because the compassion for Alanna's limitations drove me to give even more. The problem was I had little to nothing to give myself, only half as much to give to Maria, and unfortunately, hardly anything to give to my husband, other than the strength to keep giving to the family as a whole.

～

For four years, I was pretty angry. It became exhausting. Then, someone entered my life, who without intending to, helped steer me away from that path of depletion.

In the fall of 2010, we were on a family vacation in Tahoe. From our cabin, we saw an ambulance helicopter fly over near the beach. An all too familiar sight to us, as our new life was only three years old. Doug and I spoke about hoping that whoever was inside that helicopter was ok. Within about an hour, Doug was contacted by one of his patients. A young man from Petaluma had just broken his neck – perhaps we should reach out to the family? This was too weird. One thing about a spinal cord injury – the population is fairly small, but the web is pretty thick, so people reach out when necessary.

It would be a couple of months before the boy's mother reached out directly to Alanna. They lived just a ten-minute drive north from us. We set up a time to meet to talk about all things familiar with the injury. The young man who'd been injured was not present, but his mom and sister were eager to meet and discuss any possible resources to help them navigate this difficult and catastrophic injury, an injury that would unfortunately lead to his demise the next year.

His older sister, Emily, was his caregiver, and she was very welcoming in her demeanor. We told them about a facility for physical therapy called SCI-FIT (spinal cord injury-functional integrative therapy) which he would later attend. Within a few weeks, his mom informed me of a reputable stem cell treatment for spinal cord injuries in Panama. After hearing of their experience in Panama, we decided to take the trip with Alanna. The protocol was three trips – the first for one month, then two subsequent two-week trips, six months apart. Alanna, Maria, and I went for the entire month, while Doug made two trips back and forth.

Our second trip was set for January of the following year. This time it was for two weeks, and would only be Alanna and myself so Doug and Maria wouldn't have to miss work or school. The problem, however, was that I needed someone who could help with the physical requirements of Alanna, and ideally, who knew the injury.

Devastated by the news of the young man's untimely death, we'd still kept in contact with the family, trying to become some sense of support for them. The support, however, would actually turn towards us. With a second trip to Panama planned, I asked Emily, his sister and former caregiver, if she'd consider coming with us to help with Alanna. She had no hesitation in accepting. We'd only met Emily that one time, although Doug and I had visited with her mother a few times over the months. I had asked Emily in October, and we left in January, just two days after my grandmother died.

There was something very easy about the company Alanna, Emily and I kept. We all got along well. Living for two weeks together, I learned of Emily's love for yoga, and asked her to guide me through a session as I'd never taken an official yoga class. One series of yoga stretches and I was hooked! My body responded right away, and I knew this was something I needed more of on a consistent basis. We agreed on a plan right then, that once we got back home, Emily would come to our house to do yoga with me on a regular basis, and that led right into her doing yoga with Alanna as well. Ten years later, Emily is still in our life, helping Alanna with yoga, assisted walking, and cooking. A couple of years into being part of our family, Emily would reprieve me for one night a month, allowing Doug and I to go away together for a mini vacation.

Over the course of our weekly yoga sessions, I was struck by the ease of our conversations and the similar outlook on life we had. It was through this new commitment to caring for my body and soul, for the first time since Alanna's accident, combined with being seen and heard by Emily in a way that felt as if I was looking at myself in a mirror for the first time, that I began the insatiable search to learn who I was.

CHAPTER 3

FACE: THE TRAUMA

"Our lives are determined less by our childhood
than by the traumatic way we have learned
to remember our childhoods."

James Hillman,
Archetypal Psychology: A Brief Account

As I became engrossed with anything and everything regarding human behavior, I learned new ways to search my soul for answers. One such way was through EMDR, or Eye Movement Desensitization and Reprocessing, a psychotherapeutic technique for resurfacing traumatic past memories. In just one session, I faced a memory that could be best described as my initial trauma, or my core wound.

At the age of four, my voice was stifled. My boundaries became nonexistent, and I was set on a path to care for others first. I came to believe I did not matter, and that speaking was not safe because I would not be heard nor taken seriously for what I had to say.

I had just come inside from playing on the slip and slide on the front lawn with my two older brothers, who were three and four years older than me, and their two friends. I was getting out of my bathing suit in my bedroom, and my mom was helping me get dressed. My mom was bent on one knee, holding my underpants and waiting for me to step into them. My brothers' friends were standing in my doorway gawking at me, pointing and giggling at me while I attempted to put my clothes on. This made me livid!

I was crying and screaming for them to leave. I might have just been tired and hungry, but I wanted nothing to do with getting dressed until the boys were gone. They wouldn't leave, and as a young child, I wanted my mom to intervene to get them to leave, or at least shut the door. I wanted my privacy. Reflecting on this moment, I realized I was also trying to establish some boundaries. I needed my mother to take notice of me, and the situation, and make things tolerable for me. What I received instead was zero acknowledgement from my mother. She patiently knelt in front of me with her head down, waiting for me to step into my pants and get dressed.

I needed my mother to hear and respond to my screams, my cries for privacy. I needed my mother to hear and respond to my voice! I was relying on her to come to my rescue, but she didn't make them leave, nor did she shut the door. When I needed my mother to save me from what felt like an intrusion of my privacy, I was not tended to or seen by her. Instead, she ignored my desire to create a boundary. She ignored my needs. She ignored my voice.

I was ignored.

I got dressed and life went on, but so did a ripple effect of that initial trauma throughout my childhood, my adolescence, and into my adulthood.

What I've come to understand is that in that moment, I did not feel safe. My nervous system registered this lack of safety and learned to cope with it. The problem with coping with a situation that shocks the nervous system like that, or in other words, experiencing trauma, is that it manifests into a persona. As a result, the true reflection of a person becomes suppressed, and therefore, it is rarely expressed. Only when I became vulnerable and compassionate to myself, and only when I began approaching the hard work of facing my trauma and embracing my soul, was I able to start lifting the conditioned persona up to find who I was beneath it.

The memory of my mother ignoring my needs for privacy and boundaries has stayed with me my entire life. It is a memory that has repeatedly made its way into my consciousness, as though this memory, which has always appeared to me so vividly, was my gateway into accessing a much deeper part of myself. I may have never realized that part of me if it wasn't for that EMDR session, for embarking on a journey of self-inquiry and for the practice of transformative soul work.

The seemingly innocent act of my mother ignoring my need for privacy set me up for how I would approach every aspect of my life. It instilled in me the implicit belief that I – my voice, my boundaries, my needs – did not matter. I believe that brief moment set me up for a lifetime of appeasing others. In my EMDR session, I saw myself as a young child come out of the top of my head and comfort my mother by caressing her cheeks. She, in this image, did nothing, but had the same stance I recall she had in real life – down on one knee, waiting for me to step into my underpants.

Dr. Gabor Mate says trauma is not what happens to us, but what happens *inside of us*. An event can be traumatic, but the impact it has on a person is reflected in how the nervous system reacts, and that reaction is the true trauma. It is a survival coping mechanism, but it keeps a person stuck, operating from a fixated state of perceived safety. The common states of nervous system activation (or coping mechanisms) can be fight, flight, freeze, or fawn. For example, to fight would be to react to the threat with a threat, to flee would be to run in the opposite direction, to freeze would be to panic (breathless and stiff), and to fawn would be to appease or pacify.

I adopted both the fawn and freeze response, depending on the situation. While my emotional needs were not met in my moment of hysteria at age four, there was a calmness about my mother that allowed me to eventually settle down in order to cater to her need for me to be calm and get dressed.

However, the act of being unseen and unheard in my moment of need left me with the implicit belief that I didn't matter. My needs – my voice – didn't matter, but my mother's did, as the taunting from the boys went unchecked and I proceeded to put my clothes on in their presence.

I needed my mother to take action.

Actions speak louder than words, yet if someone is not aligned with their own true self, their ability to see what actions someone else may need from them will likely fall flat. As a four-year-old, I attempted to demand privacy and boundaries the only way a young child knows, by screaming and crying, but that fell on deaf ears. What did happen was my mom appeared calm. Translation: I am loved, she's still here, just try to keep the peace. The caveat, though, is that my mother wasn't emotionally present. She was unable to align with my emotional needs because of her own disconnection from herself.

In conversations with my mom, I learned she never felt heard or seen as a child, so also came to believe her words did not matter. Ergo, the apple doesn't fall far from the tree! This is generational trauma, or the passing down of conditioned behavior from parents onto their children – the next generation. My mother developed the coping mechanisms of an invisible child. She learned not to rock the boat. However, she did have an aura about her that exuded the love that is at the core of all of us, without even realizing it. Despite my needs being ignored, I still received her love.

What I didn't receive from my mother was emotional attunement. Neither seen nor heard in my hysteria, I came to believe that I didn't matter, my words had no meaning and my needs were not important. What I did get, loud and clear in my subconscious, was generational pain. I received from her the passed-down message that words do not matter, which is why she couldn't attune to my cries for help.

My mother couldn't respond to my anguish because she hadn't connected to her own. She couldn't hear her own cries for boundaries or privacy. Not emotionally attuned to herself, how could she possibly have been there for me? She was patient while I cried and screamed, but she did not take action. The message I received was, *Don't have needs of your own, but be present to the needs of others in order to feel safe and at peace.* The irony is that I unconsciously set out to live, hoping to receive what I was giving. I hoped for peace and acknowledgment from another.

This is the human condition – each of us searching
for what we didn't receive in a moment of need.
It is the core wound.

These emotional injuries manifest into our unconscious behaviors, causing us to run on autopilot (which becomes problematic when we're not aware of the underlying havoc it can wreak on our wellbeing) and allow our emotional injuries to control our behavior. This can take on many characteristics, such as overachievement, perfectionism, fixing things, or chronic people-pleasing to feel accepted, in control of overwhelming emotions, or to push down the shame that may arise from the belief that you are not enough.

My core wound resulted in me appeasing others in order to feel safe. It was much easier for me to focus on another person than acknowledge my own pain. Thus at age four, I disconnected from the essence of who I am, began behaving in a conditioned manner, and believed my voice was not worth being heard.

To hear someone is to validate their feelings, to listen to their needs, and to honor their voice. My experiences as a child taught me to diminish the need to be heard. One time my arm was pulled out of its socket during a game of cops and robbers with my friends. I'd been the robber and was being pulled off by the cop. Apparently, the strength of my friend was more than I realized. I was crying and complaining how badly it hurt, but because there was no physical obstruction to be seen, my parents couldn't figure out what was wrong. They kept questioning my pain until they finally took me to the doctor, who validated that my arm had indeed been pulled out of its socket.

I learned not to express, not to have many needs, and to essentially not speak much. This has been validated many times in my life, one example being from when I was five years old. Chastised by my kindergarten teacher for speaking during nap time, I was put into the dark boiler room as a punishment. However, this barely phased me. I didn't feel traumatized by being put in the room. I wondered why a teacher would do this, but was more interested in the pipes and where they all went as I sat there in the dark. I wondered why some pipes

were big and others small. I fell into my imagin:
all meant or could be. The punishment itself v
validation at a young age that talking wasn't wc
to be taken from my peers while they tried to sleep, amplifying
the belief that their needs were more important than mine. *No
one listened or cared to listen.* This is the narrative I came to
unconsciously believe.

As soon as I was let out of the boiler room, I ran to the
dress-up area and began to play make-believe. My imagination
is something no one has ever been able to take away from me.
In fact, by becoming my own best friend, the one person I could
rely on to receive trust, connection, and compassion from,
I managed to survive pretty well while diminishing my own
needs. I became a very quiet child with a rich inner landscape of
curiosity, observation and imagination. The poet William Blake
said, "The imagination is not a state, it is the human existence
itself." Perhaps that's why I enjoyed being around others, for the
sake of engagement with human existence – I just didn't talk
much. I listened very keenly though. Looking, listening and
observation, or actually perception, would become a dominant
feature in my makeup.

From about four to seven years of age, I'd lie in my bed and
talk with my guides. The four of them would hang out on a white
spherical plane above my window and listen to me, and I'd listen
to them. I felt protected and seen by them, and I feel they saved
me in the long run. I think I listened to them so intently because
I felt I wasn't being listened to by those around me, so I made up
for it by hearing everything. I was comforted from this very real
occurrence (or my very strong imagination). Either way, it was
real to me, yet it only lasted as long as we lived in our first house.
When I was seven, we moved up the street to a house my father

elped build, and I never experienced that particular connection again – nor did I ever forget it.

I believe my soul was meant to go through that experience as a four-year-old, and that my compassion was actually born out of my trauma when my mother ignored my emotional needs. I believe this because in the EMDR session, I saw myself come out of the top of my head and console my mother as she knelt in front of me doing nothing. I was not, nor could I ever be, responsible for her actions, only mine. And I chose to comfort her, almost as though I intuitively knew her pain and attempted to console her.

While my voice had become stifled out of fear for the response, or a lack thereof, what I did understand intuitively was empathy and compassion. My spirit knew in that moment of trauma how to save itself through instilling in me compassion, and therefore, it gave me somewhere to put myself, putting my attention onto another, in order to have a sense of myself.

That compassion helped me survive. It helped me to know who I was while I was doing, giving, listening and witnessing for another. Once I began learning more about my conditioned behavior through Soul Work, I began remembering my true self, and I've realized that while my compassion is still in play for others, I must continue to also cultivate compassion for myself.

I've since forgiven my mother for her part in silencing my voice and setting the needs of others above my own, because she did the best she could. However, I am also aware of how my nervous system was affected by that initial trauma – I know what implicit belief was instilled when I was faced with more than I could process, not just from the boys impinging upon my privacy, but from the lack of acknowledgement I received from my mother. I realized my childhood wound came from the generational pain of emotional detachment. I was not seen nor heard, and I learned my needs did not matter.

That implicit belief continued to play out in the choices I made growing up, almost as though the part of me that wasn't heard or seen for what I needed as a four-year-old skewed my perception of what might be needed from me to make a decision as an adult. As a result, I became a witness to the needs of those around me and disassociated from my own.

CHAPTER 4

WITNESS: THE DISCONNECT

"The most common sort of lie is the
one uttered to oneself."

Friedrich Nietzsche

I was seven years old. Hiding behind the couch. Scared of the yelling.

I was scared of the accusation, while I also had an unexplained sense that what was being displayed by my father was bravado, humiliation, and his own confusion. This is what I recall, but I was only seven. I didn't say anything, nor did I have the wherewithal to express this perspective. I just sat and watched. I was witness to the chaos, but never had recourse to talk about what happened.

It was about my oldest brother, Tony. We had company over, and my dad was told that Tony, just twelve years old at the time, had been caught selling marijuana. To this day, I don't know if this was ever true, but on hearing the news, my dad began reprimanding my brother in front of everyone present. I remember my brother defending himself. I never learned all the details. I just remember the disarray surrounding it and the fear I

₁elt over my dad reprimanding my brother in front of his guests. I can only imagine that my dad was trying to "do the right thing" by reacting to this news and taking control of the situation. Toward me, my dad wasn't an overbearing authoritarian parent, but the relationship between him and Tony was a different story.

I was caught by my mom when I began to smoke pot. I was carrying a bong up the street with a friend and Mom saw me throw it into the bushes. She told me to retrieve it, which I did, and I gave it to her. I was never reprimanded. I wasn't even made to go home. I heard her show it to my dad and older brother the next morning, and yet, I was never confronted. This was another unconscious validation that I didn't matter. I was "the good girl" in the family. The baby and the only girl, I could do no wrong. Even if I did, it didn't seem to matter. Even when I purposely got a bad grade, it didn't matter. However, when my brother got a bad grade, he was told to do better.

When I was twelve and began using weed, I quit the extracurricular activities I enjoyed. I danced from age four to twelve and swam competitively from age six to fifteen. When I quit, I was never questioned nor encouraged to rethink my decision. This was both a blessing and a curse. It allowed me to make my own decisions, but it resulted in me quitting things that actually brought me life and fed my soul. I think I quit those activities because none of my friends were involved in them, and instead joined in the activity that numbed me and allowed me to be with my friends.

I enjoyed getting high. It offered me an escape from things I couldn't understand and had no one to talk to about, not even in family therapy. It allowed me to go into my mind and see things more clearly. I was able to get an uncluttered view of reality, and became calmer because of it, creating my own safe space – without having to appease anyone in the process. I could benefit from the medicinal qualities and tolerate the upsets that occurred frequently while I was growing up.

As a young girl, I witnessed plenty of life's ups and downs. I learned early on to appease others and be "the good girl" to make the lives of others easier and the dynamic of our family less chaotic. I made sure I didn't cause any problems – problems that could be detected anyhow – because problems and crises were second nature to our family, and I certainly couldn't add to that.

When I was twelve years old, my oldest brother was given a mental illness diagnosis. Our paternal aunt and great aunt were also considered mentally ill. I always wonder, without a DSM diagnosis, which even some psychiatrists have said are man-made evaluations to medicate people, what kind of world it would be if the highly sensitive, creative, empathic individuals were seen for their gifts, rather than for their perceived "disturbances" that don't fit into our highly conditioned world of trauma.

Along with my brother's diagnosis were years of episodes that caused conflict and confusion within the family, with no real answers other than to medicate him. This type of upset and lack of understanding, due to poor communication, was something common that I grew up with from an early age. It was essentially emotional neglect, the type of neglect where things were rarely explained. Chaos arose and people just reacted. The professionals came in the form of psychiatrists and therapists. Nothing drastic ever changed though.

We went to family therapy to try and gain understanding, but I never spoke in those sessions. Had the therapist been any good, she would have been perceptive enough to question why the youngest was so silent when so much confusion, conflict, and frustration was running our household. I was silent because

I couldn't add to the chaos – that would mean I had needs. My unconscious conditioning had me believing I didn't have needs, nor was I worthy of having them, because when I needed comfort, attention, or someone to listen, I didn't receive it.

At the age of twelve, when my grandmother died, I started realizing what was important. I was so shaken by her death and curious about what it meant to die, and what happened after life, that I started seeing life differently. I wasn't as concerned with the normal material desires of that age – though I did have a few meltdowns if I couldn't get my hair just right! I was always very curious about what I didn't know, but not being a big conversationalist, I didn't have anyone to really talk about the mysteries of life with. I went internal for a lot of this time and saw life as an opportunity to ask hard questions. I rarely initiated this type of conversation, but I wasn't shy if the opportunity to engage in one arose, which was less often than not.

I recall visiting my great aunt sometime during my teenage years. It would be the last time we would see her as she was near death. I remember my mom having a very superficial conversation with her. I asked her why she didn't say anything to her aunt about how she was feeling about dying. I was still at the age that I didn't initiate those conversations, even though I thought about them often. My mom said something along the lines of, "You just don't talk about those things."

I was so rattled by why things like this were not commonly spoken about, especially with the dying. Perhaps that's why I took an internship in college working with terminally ill children at UC Davis Medical Center. Or perhaps it's why I worked as an aide in high school with peers who were on the Autistic Spectrum. There's always been a part of me that feels most alive when I'm interacting with people around the raw aspects of life.

Something about being in the thick of life with others makes me feel closer to God. I've no idea if this comes from growing up in a family where life and death always seemed to be on the line.

When I was fifteen, my second oldest brother was diagnosed with cancer. Misdiagnosed three months earlier, it had now spread to other parts of his body. He was in surgery for fourteen hours the day after his diagnosis. My father, just a week before my brother's diagnosis, had opened a new business since selling the pharmacy he'd partially owned for twenty-five years. He began selling metal detectors under an alter ego he developed named Jimmy Sierra. So, after three years of consistently dealing with the ups and downs of Tony's mental illness and his numerous stays in and out of treatment centers, we now had Jimmy's cancer and two years of chemotherapy to navigate, plus my parents had just opened a brand-new business. Did I mention how marijuana saved me?!

At fifteen, I was still a "good girl," not rocking the boat, but trying to offer my help however I could for my family. That meant doing what I deemed was expected of me. Show up, take up the slack, clean up, and help wherever and whenever necessary. I learned the only way to feel like I mattered was to be a good girl at home – and do whatever I wanted when not. In a way, it was kind of a good balance at that age. I had a lot of freedom, but very little external direction. I housed a lot of pain that I was unaware of, but maintained it by numbing myself to it.

Through all the ups and downs in my home life, a normalcy tried to be maintained. We went on vacations when possible and my basic needs were always met. Still, when emotional needs are not met, the psyche will search for ways to have them met, whether or not they are in the best interest of the person. As I learned at age four, my words and actions didn't really matter, unless of course, I was doing something to serve another. I was filled with so much pain – unbeknownst to me from not being seen or heard – that I could, and still can, easily see another's pain, which is why I approach others from a place of compassion. I can see and hear them more clearly than I see and hear myself. Compassion came easily for me, while self-compassion was a foreign concept.

If I unconsciously felt I didn't matter, I made sure that other people did. I took care of those I cared about and enjoyed showing my appreciation for them. At Christmas, I overdid it with gifts for my family and I loved taking gifts to my friends and their families for the holidays. At high school graduation, I made a point of getting flowers for all my friends. It was an internal expression of my genuine love and appreciation for the people who mattered to me, and it brought me a sense of peace.

Peace is what I strived for. If I could make another's life a little bit easier, without any attachments on my part, I experienced peace. This is my compassionate side. Sometimes I care too much, more than others do for themselves. It's a constant push and pull of wanting the best for others and seeking safety for myself.

Having two brothers with significant health issues made me an expert in dealing with crises by the time my mom was diagnosed with cancer when I was eighteen. The weed helped me then, too. Or so I thought. I can't remember if it was before or after my mom's diagnosis, but Tony, my oldest brother, had a psychotic break that put him in a mental hospital for a while.

I remember the day clearly. Going home from school, heading towards our long driveway, I saw a cop car in the middle of the street. My brother was in the back seat. My mom had called the cops because she didn't know what to do. Our family pet was no longer with us. My mom, in shock, was watching her son be driven off by officers, and at the same time, was trying to keep me from going into the house to see Loki in the hallway. She took me over to the other side of the house, outside, and very calmly told me what had happened. I just remember sitting there numb, not even knowing how to react. By this time in my life, I had been witness to so much pain and tragedy within my family that I was disassociated from witnessing myself. I just felt numb to it all.

I always had a compassionate place in my heart for my brother and what he must have been going through, and at the same time, I was confused about what he was going through. It never seemed like the systems in place actually helped him, other than to keep him medicated, which in the long run, was really just a way of helping those around him. If he was medicated, he was "safe" to himself, and therefore, presumably to others. It was a very frustrating and disempowering state of affairs to witness.

In my anger, frustration, and lack of understanding with all that surrounded him and his state of mind, I found it hard to communicate with my brother. So much of the communication in the house was reactionary rather than responsive. While attempts were made to gain understanding and get professional help, to me, it never seemed worthwhile. Maybe it was my age, but then again, I just sat back and witnessed. I was never a part of any problem solving or understanding. All I really knew was his medication needed to be taken, and when he went off it there was usually an episode that would put him into a "rehab" facility where we'd spend weekends visiting him. Tony always appeared present and communicative during those visits. The drugs kept him manageable.

Regardless of the hardships that played out consistently in my family, I held on tightly to potential and possibility. I kept myself above water and never succumbed to despair, despite the pain I managed to endure. I had an active social life and a boyfriend throughout my high school years. He was a best friend who stood by me through all the ups and downs.

I always knew I was the witness to the pain and tragedy my family faced. I was not the receiver of the illness or diagnosis, but I could witness and have compassion for those who were.

CHAPTER 5

ACKNOWLEDGE:
THE ROLE OF RELATIONSHIPS

"No human relation gives one possession in another
—
every two souls are absolutely different.
In friendship or in love, the two side by side
raise hands together to find what one cannot reach
alone."

Kahlil Gibran, Beloved Prophet: *The Love Letters
of Kahlil Gibran and Mary Haskell and Her Private
Journal*

As a Sagittarian, I could be stereotyped as someone who
can't or doesn't stay in relationships, jumping ship the first time
anything gets too serious. The truth is, and maybe it's my Libra
moon, I really enjoy being in a relationship. I've only had two
serious long-term relationships my entire life. Commitment is
something I take very seriously. It can feel like too much structure
and responsibility at times, but it can also fulfill a soul contract

as well as nurture life beyond our own, through our kids and our extended families.

Untethered and "Free"

There were only about four years of my young adult life where I wasn't in a committed relationship. While this short time seemed to revolve around casually dating or having a somewhat longer, yet unsustainable relationship, it was a time of exploration and learning what and who I was attracted to, and why. During this untethered period, I felt free. I was attracted to men who fulfilled my desire for play, adventure, and deep conversation. It was a time in my life that felt like, as I once told a friend, an out of body experience. I think I felt this way because I was actually living in alignment with a freer side of myself, as opposed to a more conditioned way of being, which was more quiet, complacent, and easy going.

I cherished my freedom and the desire to play and be adventurous, but I also knew it wasn't a sustainable way for me to interact with the world and get what I ultimately needed, which was someone who grounded me and took a more responsible role in achieving the practical elements of life, such as planning for the future, a family, and building a life together. That's not to say adventure and play can't exist in a responsible, practical life. Having fun can balance practicality nicely.

Finishing up community college and transferring to Sacramento State University, I was happy when I chose a major. I asked myself what made me smile, and I thought *kids, kids make me smile because of their innocence and spontaneity.* So, I chose to major in Child Development, which Sacramento State had a good reputation for. School was my main focus during those years. I was interested in studying, more than in high school, because I was able to choose my courses.

My high school boyfriend and I had broken up a year into community college. We'd dated for a little over four years. A grade older than me, he was in his second year at UC Davis. I enjoyed being in a relationship with him. He made me feel safe, grounded, and able to be myself. Our relationship confused some people as he was the ultimate extrovert, and I was the introvert, but it worked great for us. We grew up together, but eventually grew apart for reasons necessary for our own further evolution. When we finally broke up, he told me to watch out for "the guys out there." We ended the relationship as friends. He didn't want me to be taken advantage of, and I made sure I wasn't. I was twenty years old, and I was not in a committed relationship for the first time since I was fifteen-and-a-half years old –a new experience for me!

While at community college, I still had a core group of high school friends I socialized with. Being an introvert, I didn't make new friends easily, but did manage to befriend a few new people. It was always easier to make friends with guys for some reason, they just seemed more available to get along with. Because I didn't smile much, girls tended to see me as stuck up. It's easier to judge another based on how they behave rather than be curious about their behavior and the roots behind it.

After living in Lake Tahoe for the summer (a month before transferring to Sacramento State) I met a man at a wedding and spontaneously spent the next three weeks with him. We spent the majority of our time together throwing all caution to the wind. I felt free, alive, and smart enough to know it wouldn't go anywhere beyond those few weeks together before I started school again. I did, however, attempt to stay connected, hoping for more of a friendship than anything, but in the world I entered with him, it was more of a love 'em and leave 'em arrangement. I entered the affair fully knowing this, but with a side dish of fairytale hope for the possibility of something more.

I went to Sacramento State to finish my degree with the mindset of school only – get in, get out, and don't get sidetracked. This mentality, and my introverted ways, had me heading home every weekend for the first few months of attending school. I hated being alone in a strange place with nothing to do. Eventually, I got tired of making the drive for no other reason than to leave school. I had some friends from home who also attended Sac, so I began spending time with them, but I also liked the idea of not being known by many. Somehow, it gave me permission to feel free and unattached and not responsible to anyone but myself.

Doing for myself for the sake of being fully autonomous was such a strange concept to me. It was hard to feel totally relaxed and safe in my own company without needing to put my attention on another. At the same time, I did enjoy my own space and being creative with how I designed where I lived, which was primarily my bedroom while at school.

We were about to have a test in class one day and a sudden wave of disconnect and discomfort came over me. I told the teacher I wasn't feeling well, although I couldn't name what was happening to me. I took myself to the student clinic, and on my way there, a young man tripped and fell, dropping his books. As everyone kept walking onward and around him, I stopped and helped him get his books. Even amidst my own panic attack, I stopped and helped someone else, because putting attention outside of myself and onto another was always more natural for me. It gave me a sense of self, safety, and comfort.

By the time I got to the clinic, I had to wait to be seen. While I waited, still unsure of why I was even there, a very tall, husky man wearing a white t-shirt came walking toward me. The words were yellow and couldn't be read from afar except for one word in red, in the middle of his shirt, which said, "scared". When he got closer to me, I could see the entire message was "Don't be scared of me." An African American man, his message was addressing systemic racism. He sat right next to me with a big smile, and we began talking. There was an energy about him that made me feel comfortable. His presence, demeanor, and conversation gave me a sense of safety.

Between our conversation and my meeting with someone from the clinic, only to hear nothing more than they didn't think anything was wrong with me, I felt more seen and understood by the stranger I'd just met in the waiting room. He became a fast friend and a person who was safe for me to be myself around. We spent a decent amount of time together exploring each other's worlds. The fast pace of the relationship also gave me some extreme anxiety in the beginning. I felt like I dove into something that, while it felt comfortable, also scared the crap out of me.

I remember going to my assigned supervisor in the Child Development department out of desperation. I wanted so badly for her to read my mind, to know what I had just got myself into with a total, yet familiar, stranger. I wanted her to tell me that all was ok. I wanted her to see the distress on my face that I could find no words to explain. My new friend brought a connection that I apparently desperately needed to feel grounded, but it also brought me great inner turmoil because I didn't know why I was so drawn to this person. I didn't know how to emotionally take care of myself in an environment that brought up so much emotion, ultimately, because I was alone. The emotional neglect from childhood didn't prepare me for being totally alone, feeling like I had little sense of myself unless I was in a relationship with another.

For a short time, this relationship filled a need I had to feel connected to someone. It was as though I was better able to contact myself through the eyes of another, as a result of disassociating from myself at four years old, when my sense of self, in a relationship, had been hijacked. I unconsciously learned that who I was had to do with how I connected to someone else in a relationship. For me, that was most often about what I could do for another, about getting some satisfaction around serving them. For example, I enjoyed buying my high school boyfriend gifts. Giving to others is how I learned to give credence to myself, and being in casual, non-committal relationships, although freeing, amplified the loneliness ingrained in me as a child even further. I yearned to be committed to another because I yearned to be committed to myself.

Marriage

It was a hot summer's day. I was on foot, making my way around the corner, approaching the long and winding road ahead of me as I walked home. There he was. He pulled up to the stop sign in his tan VW bug. I remember the fleeting thought that raced through my mind. *That's your husband. You will spend your life with him.* It was such a fast thought, more of a message, but one I clearly remember having. I was about fourteen years old at the time.

Eight years later, our mutual friend was getting married. It was another hot day in summer. As I walked in a pair of tiny heels from the gravel parking lot to the church, I thought, *Okay Ang, you're ready to meet someone. The time is right.*

I was met with a slight bow and a comment, two steps up to the entrance of Saint Anselm's church, "Wow, well you've certainly grown up." I giggled uncomfortably and smiled. His name was Doug. As one of the groomsmen, he asked me, "Can I walk you to your pew?"

The reception took place at The Falkirk mansion, a beautiful landmark nestled away from the street with a massive, manicured grassy area leading up to the grand estate room. The staircase and fire mantel draped with warmth, the wooden architecture felt home to many stories and gatherings.

Our mutual friend was a family friend, so both our families were there. As guests were arriving, we gathered at the bar and my dad proceeded to tell all sorts of stories, which is a gift of his. He caught Doug's ear, and they shared words until the food was served.

Any good wedding has a dance floor, and that's where Doug and I found our groove together. We danced and had fun, being moved by the music and enjoying each other's company. Our mothers, standing on the sidelines watching us, talked the entire time.

Doug and I seemed to fall into each other's company fairly easily. I think we both just rode the wave we were on together. He asked me to go with him to the after party at the brother of the groom's house. It was there my heart fell in love with his.

I didn't consciously know then that I would be with Doug for life, but it did feel like I was home. It wasn't like fireworks went off – it was more of an inner smile that resonated with his heart. I was certainly attracted to him, and there was something that felt comfortable about him. As he straddled a picnic bench, he spoke of his puppy, Nikki. I felt the love he had for his dog, and that's what I fell in love with – his ability to feel love. Something in me, something that wasn't a conscious choice, felt at peace with him. We went for a walk down the dark moonlit street and I listened to him talk of the dreams he had for his future, one being that he wanted to go to Tahiti for his honeymoon. Disconnected from my own needs, it was harder for me to envision my dreams of the future. Therefore I listened to his, not adding much when he asked me of mine.

The evening came to an end when he drove me home. He handed me his phone number and said, "Call me if you want to go out sometime." I guess that was his way of avoiding rejection if he made the first move and I said no. As fate would have it, the morning of the wedding I'd won tickets from the radio station, KJazz, to see Gladys Knight and the Pips, so of course I asked him if he'd like to go with me. The rest is history.

It's funny how things work out. I believe in divine order, even when we don't see the order as it unfolds. When I went to my friends' wedding, I had the thought that I was ready to meet someone, and less than five minutes later, I met the man I would marry just two years later. Doug and I felt pretty comfortable with each other from the get-go and quickly became a source of support for each other. Our first year together was spent long distance from each other, as Doug was in his last quarter at Palmer College of Chiropractic West, in Santa Clara, and I had one more year at Sacramento State University.

After graduating college, I went to Europe for five weeks. The day after I arrived in London, I received a call at the hotel. It was Doug, asking if I wanted to go to Hawaii with him upon my return. When I got back from Europe, I had two days to wash my clothes and repack for a ten-day trip to Hawaii to stay with Doug's friends from high school.

That trip brought a marriage proposal. Not quite the one Doug had in mind, nor one I was definitely expecting, but I did have a strong intuition it was going to take place. On the airplane, I'd noticed a bulge in the front pocket of his backpack. Being the curious person I am, I asked him what it was. "Oh, nothing," was his response. I let it go, but was still quite curious as I wondered if it was a ring. *Why would he want to go all the way to Hawaii with me if he didn't have a long-term plan to be with me?* We'd talked about a future together, but not about how soon that future would take place.

We were at Hanauma Bay on Oahu when I said, "So, were you going to propose to me?"

Much to his surprise (and mine, quite frankly), he said, "Well, yes, I was. Will you marry me?" His original plan was to take me to a beach in Kauai, where we'd planned on going in a few days, and propose at sunset. I kind of spoiled that plan. However, when he did ask me, I froze. I didn't answer him. I knew whatever words came out of my mouth, I would stand by. For me to be certain I was making the best choice for myself, I needed time. This was a lesson for me in learning to trust myself based on what felt like the best decision I could make. I like to weigh things carefully and be purposeful with big decisions in my life.

I did say yes ... a day and a half later. Doug and I fit together in a way that seemed to make sense, as far as we knew. We were kind and respectful and enjoyed each other's company. We'd often go bike riding after work around the lakes near our home, we enjoyed going out to dinner, and before we had kids, we'd take weekend trips to Carmel or Lake Tahoe. The love I have for him has been the kind that feels like home, even though it's been shaken up more than a few times over the thirty-five years we've been together.

Doug's work consumed him more over the years as he dedicated to expanding his business in chiropractic care. I was raising our children, so his focus went into work. With Alanna's injury, my focus went exponentially into her care. This inevitably meant less time for our marriage and relationship. Working so much gave Doug something to do instead of grieving, and a distraction from losing me to Alanna's needs.

After years of intensive caretaking, then diving into Soul Work, finding my voice, and pursuing my passions, I began to see all the dysfunction in our relationship. My insatiable curiosity kept me leaning in to discover more truths I was unaware of, but kept showing up for. This brought up tension in the marriage because we weren't on the same page. Doug was coping by distraction – I was coping through caretaking. I began doing the work to address why. For us to conquer our conflicts, he needed to do the work for himself as well. We have since acknowledged the role of conditioned behavior in our relationship and continue to work through the dysfunction that arises between us as a result. We are in a great place now, with a better understanding of each of ourselves, us together, and the reasons why things manifested as they did.

Relationships are funny and beautiful places for healing if the couple takes on the challenge when things get tough. For me, our relationship has not had the feelings of fireworks or fairytale scenarios, but has been a relationship based on a feeling of deep love. Despite the rocky moments that have arisen, as with any relationship, we keep coming back to each other one layer stronger.

Doug and I renewed our vows after twenty-five years of marriage. For our second wedding, I did it my way – on a beach in Maui, with my parents and our daughters there to witness. We initially got married at the church where he and I met. I'd never envisioned a church wedding, but I did it for my mother, knowing how important it was to her. I hadn't been accustomed to honoring my own needs based solely on what I wanted.

Yes, of course, the marriage was my choice, but more times than I was ever aware of, I neglected or diminished my own needs in place of putting others first. Usually, this was for someone in my family or someone I cared deeply for. I would come to learn in my fifties how I'd been unconsciously conditioned in my childhood to appease others first before considering my own needs. I had to first embark on a journey of self-reflection so I could acknowledge the role of other people's needs in my life and embrace my own.

By taking an intimate perspective, I've realized I lost a sense of fun, adventure, and spontaneity as I sought to feel grounded and responsible in a committed relationship. I became more complacent with others taking control. During the short time in my college years that I was not in a committed relationship, I felt very much at choice, which I was, with who and how I spent my time. I felt the way I interacted with young men was an exploration of what was important to me, what left me feeling alive in a relationship, what didn't, and what filled a particular role.

However, I had no idea my inability to access my deeper emotions, the ones that were trying to tell me I was ok on my own, that what I needed was inside me and no one else was going to fill that void, kept me in an unconscious loop of searching for "the one" who would put me at ease. While I casually dated, I knew within a very short time if a person was a fun-factor with a side of seduction or a serious candidate for a lifelong relationship.

Like I said before, when I went to my friend's wedding, I told myself I was ready to meet someone. And that I did. Once I was in a committed relationship, I fell right back into functioning on autopilot and yielding my power to make decisions to someone else, rather than relying on myself.

It's understandable, and yet ironic, that the partner I chose shares similar traits to my mother. This is totally normal for many couples. We're drawn to the "familiar" in a relationship. This can become problematic, as I discovered, when one partner goes inward and begins to dismantle their conditioned behavior. To be in an intimate relationship with someone whose traits are similar to those of the person who initiated the core wound and implicit beliefs can make for a future together that either fits, because it's "familiar" and feels right, or cause conflict when the doors open into a deep-dive of self-exploration and truth. The couple can either create a more intimate bond if both parties agree to exist in the reality of "what is", or they can become triggered into a reactive state. The former undoubtedly takes practice and patience, but the willingness to show up for oneself first allows a much more tender relationship to ultimately evolve over time.

Our Wedding Vows ~ September 24, 1988

"I join with you today to allow our friendship to grow. To give and receive life in good times and in bad, for richer or poorer, in sickness and in health. To always respect and honor your being as a precious gift that you shared with me. To bring you joy with each new day, and to love you from the depth of my soul, so that we may never part so far as to forget the mystery and wonder of this beautiful love that life has given us."

My Reflections on our Vows ~ Thirty Years Later

I took a sacred vow to love you, Douglas DeSalvo,
For better and for worse, Through good times and
bad, Through sickness and in health.

These are universal vows, because whomever wrote
them knew that marriage is work – it is not a cake
walk – it is a marathon that takes stamina to make
it through.

Stamina, in anything, requires a clear intention in
order to know where the focus needs to be.

My intention in my marriage with you is to rise
after I fall and continue to become the best I can
be – in becoming who I need to be for me – in
loving me in my dark parts and my struggles,
allowing me to become more of myself and contact
my joy and pleasure and birthright of living with,
and in desire of, all that life can offer. I want to be
ready and willing to receive opportunities in life as
they are presented to me.

I am working through my struggles in becoming
the person I want to be, and deserve to be, and am
capable of being in terms of having a viable business
and sharing my offerings with the world.

These struggles for me bring up very real obstacles
and fears around being seen, being heard, being
appreciated, being vulnerable, being wrong, being
appeasing, being righteous.

And I am at the precipice of having faced all these fears in order to know who I am at my core, and because I led, often times unaware, with the intention of wanting more for myself and wanting answers to things I did not know, I paved the way for my soul – my core being, the truth of who I am – to be revealed to me.

In continuing with my fierce determination of intention – to be all of me – I walked through the fire with my own demons in order to become the woman I am, so close to sharing with the world, in order to be an instrument for others who wish to discover the truth of who they are.

In my marriage to you, finding the truth of who I am might have its detrimental effects if I don't also see the truth of who you are.

This is where I am responsible for how I show up for you.

I cannot be responsible for how you receive me, if my intention is pure and kind and coming from an open heart.

This is my work to stay open to myself – to stay open to myself – to stay open to myself, in order for me to be open to all of you.

The vows include sickness, bad and worse, because we are not perfect beings. We are human, and being better, good and healthy, is not possible all the time.

If it were, self-care would not be so critical to humans who wish to manifest and cultivate happiness, joy, pleasure, and gratitude, which are inherent to our being; which are, in our essence, our birthright; which are the truth of who we are.

We just need to face the bad, sick, and worse parts of ourselves in order to remember and reclaim the truth of who we are, and in that we get to be the full expression of healthy, good, loving human beings that we hopefully get to share in the sacred union of marriage.

CHAPTER 6

EMBRACE:
THE COMPASSIONATE CAREGIVER

"I feel the capacity to care is the thing which gives
life its deepest significance."

Pablo Casals

One year into our marriage, Doug was running his own successful chiropractic office and I was working at a non-profit business. After a year at that job, I worked for my parents while I went to night school to get my teaching credential. A year later, we bought our first house. After finishing my schooling and student teaching, I got pregnant. With a degree in Child Development and a teaching credential, I went on to work at a preschool and teach swimming to young kids before, and during, my pregnancy. Doug and I agreed that when I gave birth, I'd be a stay-at-home mom. While I dabbled in part-time side jobs during motherhood, being a mother to my two daughters has been THE greatest joy of my life.

We had our first daughter, Alanna, in our fifth year of marriage. I had a miscarriage when Alanna was two years old, then gave birth to Maria, our second daughter, a year later.

The story of Alanna's labor and delivery was forty hours long. After two days of prodromal labor and no progress (I never dilated past four centimeters), I was prepped for a C-section. With the drape laid in front of me and my hands strapped down (this being the procedure, I guess, so I wouldn't rip the drape down that separated the mother from the unnatural, yet lifesaving procedure of cutting the child out of her womb), the doctor had just announced he was about to make the incision.

"Wait, I'm having a contraction! Can I do some pelvic lifts first?" I asked.

"Well, that would be very surprising if you can," he said, "as you should be numb from the procedure of the epidural." But there I was, doing pelvic raises on the operating table, so the doctor yelled out the door that the patient, me, needed, "Stadol, STAT!" Apparently, I wasn't numb enough, and somehow my unborn child knew that and saved me from experiencing the agonizing pain of my womb being cut into. Had that occurred, I would have been knocked out immediately with stronger drugs and would not have been present for Alanna's birth, assuming I would have survived it.

When they were sewing me back up, I had to say to the nurse, "What if I throw my child out the window? What if I just don't know what to do, and I do something terrible?" I had to know everything was going to be okay – I was being sent home with a human being I was supposed to raise, no instructions included. Thank goodness my maternal instincts kicked in and I took on the job of motherhood wholeheartedly. Three-and-a-half years later, I was able to have a VBAC (vaginal birth after caesarean) with Maria, after two days of prodromal labor, just as before with Alanna. This time, though, we were back home within twenty-four hours of me giving birth.

I value honesty and authenticity, and I strived to raise my girls with these values. Of course, my husband and I co-parented together, but I think, with many couples whose roles are breadwinner and stay-at-home caretaker, the one who spends the most time with the children is the one who ultimately creates the tone for messaging. That's not to say Doug had less influence on our children, just less time invested in actually raising them. As a result, I acquired a better pulse on the flow and makeup of their personalities. I can see how this can become a double-edged sword for the breadwinner. Less time with their children creates a different relationship overall, not better or worse, just different.

Because I was a stay-at-home mom, I got to run on my own rhythm, while of course creating a structure for my girls. This left time, especially when they were young, to live each day within a flow of creativity, replicating that feeling of adventure and spontaneity I'd experienced years before. The girls and I had the freedom to drive to Sonoma with friends for a day at Train Town or to Sausalito to explore the Discovery Museum. Our days were filled with fun activities that helped to foster creativity and exploration. I enjoyed creating crafts to do at home, from making cookie dough ornaments to picking leaves from the yard and creating place mats out of them. We had an easel in the garage for art when the feeling hit, and art projects were a regular occurrence.

While the domestic duties were regularly attended to, it felt like play was easily accessed on any particular day and living in the moment was the first order at hand. Alanna began attending preschool a couple of days a week at age two-and-a-half. My rhythm then could be defined by a slow pace. If there wasn't any place for me or the girls to be in the morning, it was easy to stay in our pajamas and play until late morning. While Alanna was in school, Maria liked to role play with her dolls, or with me, telling me, "I'm the mommy and you're the sweetheart." We would have an entire conversation like this with a make-believe trip to the hospital to have a baby. Dress up was always a way for the girls to explore life through their imagination and the roles they were playing.

We have countless videos of the girls playing dress up with each other, their friends, and their cousins. One such home video is of a marriage ceremony being played out with a close friend's son when Alanna and Maria were three and six years old. Many of the costumes they used came from the dancing days of my youth. I believe that watching them play, and also playing alongside them, kept me in the enjoyment of being a mom. I received joy in watching my girls create. My own sense of creation became putting their needs, wants and desires first and doing what I could to hopefully give them a fun and enjoyable childhood.

I was involved in my daughters' formative school years when it came to chaperoning field trips. I think both girls enjoyed me going on field trips with them. I was an unspoken safe place for them, at least that was my perception, and I didn't sense any signs that it wasn't ok for me to be there. I have two distinct memories from those trips. We were driving home from a trip into the city, and I found myself on Broadway Street, in the red-light district!! I've never been great with directions. All I could think was, *Oh my god! What have I done?* and all I could do was hope the kids wouldn't look out the window. But of course, they got curious about all the flashing signs outside, and all I could say was, "Don't look!" while halfway laughing and half-horrified at what their parents might say if they found out. All turned out well though, and it was a field trip to remember – at least the ride home was, since Alanna and I have both forgotten where the field trip even took us in the first place.

The other distinct memory I have of attending a field trip was to the pumpkin patch with Maria's class. We came home with a puppy from the ranch, much to Alanna and Doug's surprise. That dog actually turned out to be a dog from hell, unfortunately.

I chose to volunteer for field trips because it fulfilled my desire for playful adventure, which I didn't often make time to curate for myself. Field trips were easy. I got to be with my kids and experience whatever the adventure was without having to plan it around myself. I could explore without having to consider where I wanted to go or what I wanted to do, which I now realize allowed me to fulfill a need I had for fun within the safe parameters of catering to other people's needs. Field trips were similar to family vacations in that regard.

Our family was fortunate enough to go on vacations a few times a year. Trips to Lake Tahoe were a yearly destination, going at least once in the summer and once in the winter. Summer times were fun, filled with camping and outdoor exploration. We went to Stinson beach for a week with my family when Alanna was only ten days old, and again with my family, to Lake Tahoe when Maria was ten days old. That means just five days after coming home from a C-section with Alanna, I was already in vacation mode.

Strangely enough, I got mastitis with both of them when they were about two weeks old. Both times, on vacation. Maybe it was more than I could handle, but I was young and just pushed through. After all, these were both trips planned by my mom.

Youth got me through it, but clearly, I was so cut off from my own needs that everyone else's took precedence. It feels strange to reflect on this, seeing how easy it was for me to go along with plans I didn't make, but ultimately enjoyed, even though with mastitis I felt like I had the flu for part of it.

When I weaned Alanna from breastfeeding, I remember a certain day she was in her crib, crying for me. I thought she wanted to nurse, so I let her cry, and later, took in a bottle. I was trying to wean the daytime nursing. In the end, I gave her the choice between me and the bottle. She chose the bottle, and that was it. I did the same thing with Maria, but was more relaxed with the time frame.

I raised my first-born child with the belief I was "doing it right", that I was attending to her needs and listening to her innate rhythm of what worked and what didn't. From my perspective, keeping her safe, while also trying to honor her individual being, was important, but my conditioned idea of safety was tending to the needs of others, despite my own.

I have to wonder if this is how I may have taken Alanna's voice away from her, because as a first-time mother, I imparted what I felt was right in certain situations. What felt right to me stemmed from the implicit beliefs that I've only recently been able to recognize were a result of generational trauma. I wonder if my comfort in being more isolated inhibited Alanna in her social development. It's not as though she wasn't socialized, or that I was a hermit. She was going to preschool at two-and-a-half years old, and we had plenty of play dates with other moms. But her demeanor did change at the age of three, after my miscarriage. She became more reserved, yet obstinate, as she was always a strong-willed child. Could it have been she took on the grief of my miscarriage, giving her an unconscious belief around abandonment?

Alanna saw us, her parents, on an equal playing field. She was always an outwardly loving child. When the theme song to Barney came on she would go up to anyone present and give them a big hug. She was a very wise young child, and very sensitive. Both my girls were, and still are. It was harder for me to see that, objectively, at times when they were growing up. I think this is what happens when enmeshment occurs, which can be easy when we take on the role of responsibility over others to an extreme.

I now realize how easy it is to cross boundaries of individual sovereignty while having to be the parent who guides from experience. Attuned to their strengths, I encouraged them both to harness them. Alanna's love of movement was channeled into dance, and Maria channeled her love of playing with others into soccer. Alanna enjoyed dancing from age three to twelve, the same time frame I had. A broken arm and chicken pox took her out of two different recitals, and then she slowly phased it out.

Alanna was in a karate class at four years old. One day, she had to be tested on a sequence of poses. The teacher approached her as though she wasn't going to pass because of her quiet nature and lack of engagement, but much to his surprise, Alanna knew the entire sequence. She advanced to the next belt, but decided the loud nature of the sport wasn't for her, and she stopped. Her demeanor, while being a fiery Aries, is quite docile.

Alanna is a listener. I am as well, despite being a Sagittarius, which is considered a lively sign. Alanna's fire and my passion for life are more internal traits of ours. We can come across as quiet due to our introspective natures, and because less talking is done, people can assume us to be aloof or disinterested. I can see here where the generational trauma was passed down. I do believe I was tuned in to her being, but I couldn't possibly be everything for her, and yet, because of my implicit programming, I still feel like I was supposed to be.

Alanna's first day of kindergarten was met with Doug and me, along with all the other parents and younger siblings, walking her into class and visiting, probably longer than was necessary. It was a new structure for all of us and we needed to ease into it, so the school allowed for short morning gatherings. Fast forward three years to Maria's first day in kindergarten, and she couldn't get out of the car fast enough, running to her class and yelling with excitement, "I got this! I can do it myself!"

Maria is my social butterfly who always wanted to be fiercely independent. She, although being a more innately quiet Cancer, was more adamant about her desires and claimed her independence early on. As I did for Alanna, I put Maria in dance classes at the age of three, but it didn't take long to realize that wasn't for Maria. While she stayed with it for about a year, she was entirely more interested in being social than she was in learning how to do tap or ballet. Soccer became Maria's favorite extracurricular activity from the age of five to ten. I was her coach for three of those years, although I'd never played the game. Once she reached the age when keeping score counted, I bowed out of being a coach.

～

When Alanna broke her neck and became instantly paralyzed in a state across the country, our world was turned upside down and forcefully shaken in all directions. One day, my daughters were getting ready to attend their cousin's wedding together, primping themselves in the mirror, playing with makeup and wearing high heels because they could. Six hours later, life as we knew it drastically changed.

Alanna's accident in Florida brought us back home to California a week later, but it didn't bring Alanna or me back to our house. Instead, we went to Oakland Children's Hospital for rehab and further evaluation of her new injury. This is where we began to learn what her injury really meant for Alanna. Broken neck, paralyzed, quadriplegic, *unable to...* were the new words, concepts, and realities in our new lives. These were hard realities that needed time to sink in, even though we were required to face the reality of "what is" on a minute-to-minute basis. Everything is always in flux, and yet the unknowns of change can make "what is" feel like a hopeless, bottomless pit of despair.

The way I see it, once I have my bearings of what is occurring in the moment, I have a choice of how to approach the unknown. As scary and uncertain as the unknown can look and feel, there is an inner force bigger than each of us that can ultimately choose between stagnancy or movement forward towards a path of growth, possibility, and potential. This is the mindset I took on when I witnessed my first-born child lose the function of her body. I was in denial, maybe. In fact, Alanna has gotten through her life denying much of this injury. At least the parts she can. She was at the will of her injury, along with her own tenacity. And me, I was at the will of survival and doing all I could to keep my family together, while also being a solid, insurmountable force to Alanna and her condition.

Being an insurmountable force felt like a pretty tall order, but I entered into the position of full-time caregiver as though it were second nature to me, and it kind of was, just not to the extent I'd ever experienced before.

It is unfathomable to think what it would be like to experience the aftermath of a catastrophic injury to your own child – until you do. Conceptually, it's not too hard to imagine. But to live it is a whole other ball game. For me and my spouse, to suddenly be met with so many unknowns when it came to life as we knew it being tossed out the window – along with the ideas or dreams we had for Alanna, let alone her own dreams for herself – caused us to search. The shock, the denial, the tenacity, and the perseverance with what was occurring, along with the support of the community, all helped to propel us as a family to go forward.

Alanna's injury brought about a life I never imagined, and yet there I was, attending it, fully conscious of my decision to be her caregiver but losing myself in it at the same time. I was used to showing up in crises. It's as though I was trained to learn how to perpetually exist in one. If all is in divine order, was my past training in crisis management – the diagnoses, prognoses, turmoil, tragedy, and death of family members – meant to be put to use for my daughter's future? I believe it was.

My core wound from childhood instilled compassion in me, and being unshakeable in the face of crises, comfortable as a caregiver and primed for appeasement, with the desire to serve others ingrained in me, gave me the strength to take on this new life with responsibility and determination. Beginning a new life as a fifteen-year-old confined to a wheelchair because of paralysis, with total dependence on others, is a massive obstacle to endure. But this is the story of my journey, and Alanna's is her own to share. I can say, however, that she and I both had our learning curves, as did the whole family.

Maria's more social personality seemed to make the transition a little easier for her. It would take me two years, however, to learn that Maria was having panic attacks in middle school. I was always concerned for Maria after Alanna's injury. I knew from my own life that the quiet, agreeable one is usually the one who needs the most attention. This was Maria. I checked in with her often, but she was good at appeasing too, letting me believe that all was ok and she was fine. There was a delicate balance to uphold in allowing her the space to be able to communicate her concerns, while also helping to create that space for her. She was pretty honest with how she felt and what she needed when she made contact with her emotions, but the long-term effects on her psyche that manifested as a result of the trauma wouldn't really come out until her senior year of high school, six years post-injury.

She called me from school in the midst of a major panic attack, so I drove straight there to meet her. I suggested, since she'd planned to go off to college the following year, that perhaps it was time to go into therapy, either together or alone. She immediately decided to do it alone, and from then on, began therapy. Almost ten years later, she still appreciates therapy when she feels the need to use it.

I was there for Maria in every capacity I could be, but I know she suffered in feeling second fiddle to her sister, who required the attention when it was needed. Doug suffered as well. I was not available to give myself fully to them, as much as I gave to Alanna. It was Doug who missed out the most from me. I had little to nothing for him. In fact, it would be eleven years post-injury before we would take a trip alone for more than one night, when we went to Bali for a week to attend a yoga/music retreat.

The thing is, I too was missing out on my relationship with Maria and Doug, but I was in the hyper-giving, ultra-appeasing mode, and my conditioned behavior had me, well, conditioned. I barely recognized my own needs, or that I could even have them, when it came to growing and attending to these other two relationships. I can definitely see now how my need to appease, and the responsibilities that I took to heart, closed me off to receiving anything else, especially when it came to my own needs as an individual, mother of two, and a wife.

Statistically, 80% of marriages end in divorce when met with a catastrophic experience. We have been married thirty-four years this year, fifteen years post-injury. While there have been times of great hardship within our relationship, we've always found our way back to each other. In fact, we are stronger and at the healthiest place we've ever been in our marriage. I attribute this to couples therapy and the desire to know ourselves individually, as well as together. I am beyond fortunate to have a husband who understands the sacrifices I made as a caregiver, and who has chosen to remain faithfully by my side, despite this reality.

As life would have it, my choice to be a stay-at-home mom gave me flexibility. At the time of Alanna's injury, I was working part-time in Doug's office running the insurance department and front desk, but then taking care of Alanna became my full-time job, and an added layer to my role as her mother. I've always been a mother first and foremost to her. This is why the compassion I have for her injury has so significantly steered my choices in the direction of being her full-time caregiver. It also led to our enmeshment.

For several years following her injury, my life was only devoted to Alanna's wellbeing. Alanna was in her last week of her freshman year of high school when she was injured. For the remainder of her high school years and her first two years of college, I poured everything I had into making sure she had her needs met, and that her days as a teenager were celebrated as "normally" as possible. She wanted to come home from Shriner's Hospital ten days earlier than her release date because she wanted to be back at school for spirit week, and that she did.

For her sixteenth birthday, Alanna and her friends went to the city in a limo as we drove behind them. Alanna got her license at age seventeen, she became the senior class president, and she went to prom. She went to Disneyland for her senior trip because I took the bus down with her. She spoke at her high school graduation. Instead of this being a time when we as parents got to witness our first child become independent – driving and socializing in the ways an adolescent does – I had to be a quiet participant in her social life, ensuring she could maintain one despite her limitations, while also trying to be as invisible as I could.

For the next few years of her high school days, I drove Alanna to her physical therapy appointments. Doug had located SCI-FIT, a facility that had opened earlier in the year. The owner of SCI-FIT had broken his neck as well and opened up a gym for rehabilitating spinal cord injuries at Pleasanton. I'd pick her up from school at 2 pm and drive seventy-five minutes, she'd work out for two hours, then we'd return home at about 8 pm. We did this twice during the week, and on Saturdays, for three years. Fourteen years later, I still drive her to the same facility to work out for three hours once a week. Her other therapies are now done at home. After all these years, she's never given up going to Pleasanton for her exercise. Fortunately, they are finally opening another SCI-FIT only twenty-five minutes away from us, and Alanna now plans to take herself.

Caregiving during those four years after her injury was, for the most part, a flurry of ever-present memories, still swirling in my mind to this day. I gave, and I gave, and I gave, out of compassion for Alanna and what she was up against, but also while not realizing I was living in the familiarity of my conditioned behavior to give because "I was supposed to", and needed to in order to feel safe. I was trying to keep Alanna from feeling emotionally abandoned in my unconscious attempt to ultimately heal myself through her, whom I was projecting my own experiences onto.

I became her landing place. I wanted to give her the opportunity to still excel, and she did. She received awards in high school for being inspirational. She got into USF and graduated with a double major and honors – forty-eight hours after having an appendectomy. She held down a full-time job after graduating. She became an event manager, and is now working as a successful and passionate nutritionist. I took care of Alanna for Alanna, so she could succeed, and feel safe and comfortable, but in my conditioned state of behaving while on autopilot to appease others, I did so while foregoing my own needs. Taking care of myself was non-existent, and that was not sustainable.

I don't recall what year it was this occurred, but I'd venture to say it was in the first or second year of being Alanna's caregiver. All I remember was being in Alanna's room, helping her with something, and I snapped. I ran into my closet and crouched down in a dark corner, absolutely hysterical. Screaming and crying, I lost all sense of feeling. Or was it that I was feeling too much and couldn't process the stress? I just remember, if I had a gun, I might have used it on myself.

The mental, physical, and emotional pain was more than I could bear at that moment. Doug stood in the closet doorway, just looking at me, understandably unsure of what to do, but holding the space for me to do whatever it was I was doing. I see now it wasn't because I was Alanna's caregiver. It was more because I had never allowed myself to break, ever, in my entire life, and my appeasing ways had fully consumed me. I just "did" for others without regard for myself. I operated under the belief that I had no needs. I made a life of fulfilling others' needs.

No one can do that, even though we believe we can. That brief breakdown was an action, a plea from my nervous system to just take note. Even then, after my episode, I got back up, dusted myself off, and continued on.

Crisis is second nature to me. I am well-versed in the health crises of loved ones. Being the youngest of three children, and learning not to create strife or have problems because there were too many that needed the attention, I was given the groundwork, an apprenticeship almost, in knowing how to respond in crisis. Show up and do the work necessary. Keep with the order of business. Make things easier and more comfortable for others, and if, and only if, there's time for myself to do something other than sleep, then do it without creating waves. Sleeping was about the only thing I had time for. It wasn't until I made a connection with Emily, another caregiver I could see myself in, four years after Alanna's injury, that I began to understand what it really meant to take care of myself for the first time in my life.

Being a mother was, by choice, my full-time job. While a choice, it was also a way I unconsciously lost myself in others and put their needs before mine. I never regretted the choices I made in motherhood. However, I've come to learn that forgetting oneself in an attempt to do good by another will eventually leave something to be desired.

I love being a mom. I think in many ways I found a voice I didn't have before I became a mother. What I loved most about raising my girls was not only being there to tend to them, but also witnessing their growth as little people becoming themselves. Fast forward to my daughters as grown, young women. I couldn't be more proud of how they have approached their lives after having endured a catastrophic crisis in their formative years. Alanna has her own busy practice as a Functional Nutritionist.

Maria, after starting her own podcast and magazine titled *Mdrn Day Muse*, has left that creative endeavor for a more sustainable, yet challenging income as a real estate agent.

These young women, who I get to say are my daughters, are very wise and intuitive, and have shown exceptional growth in their abilities to be with their true selves, continuing to forge their way in the world according to their own desires and boundaries. They have become a reflection of the intentions I had as I raised them. They are strong, independent, and passion-driven women who understand hardship is a part of life and the best way through it is forward. They understand that perseverance towards any desire will ultimately manifest, and if manifestation takes longer than desired, that passion will continue to recalibrate their actions so they can live with integrity.

I love to watch the human condition unravel. That's not to say everything I did as a mother was absent from my own conditioned behavior. Unfortunately, I wouldn't learn that until later in my life, but when I did, I made apologies and addressed where my behavior was carrying down the generational pain. I hope this recognition helps to break the cycle, and that my daughters can discover their truest selves earlier in their lives than I did. That's a journey they each must embark on for themselves, although it appears they are both already well on their way. They will always have my unconditional love, but living with compassion for themselves is in their own hands, as it is for everyone to discover their true self.

CHAPTER 7

DISCOVER: TRUE SELF

"As human beings, our job in life is to help people realize how rare and valuable each one of us really is, that each of us has something that no one else has - or ever will have - something inside that is unique to all time. It's our job to encourage each other to discover that uniqueness and provide ways of developing its expression."

Fred Rogers, *You Are Special: Neighborly Wit And Wisdom From Mister Rogers*

"Mom, sometimes you're just too raw and too real and people aren't ready for that." *Oh, ok. So that's what it is,* I thought to myself.

I appreciated Alanna's raw and real insight into this reality I impose upon others. To me, this is the reason for communication – to be raw and real. It never occurred to me that people don't like this form of communication, or are simply made to feel uncomfortable by it. I used to get frustrated that people generally don't like real talk, but are more comfortable with small talk.

There's a time and place for chit chat, but I like diving into "what is". I was never comfortable with small talk, which was probably part of the reason I'd listen more than talk. I've also come to learn that is common with empaths. It's as though there's an entire world to always be tapping into, and to fill it with superficial commentary and distractions seems like a disrespect of the sacredness of life. And, on the other hand, angels fly because they take themselves lightly. I was fifteen when my friend and next-door neighbor looked at me and said, "You are so intense."

One thing I know for sure is that I am encouraged and motivated by potential – mine and yours. I believe life is made better by potential because it offers something to reach for, a vast expanse of opportunities. With the many dramatic scenarios, familial crises, and unconscious fears I've had, I've tried to direct it all into potential. Potential that would make me feel I was involved in life, not just standing by witnessing the pain of my loved ones.

I am innately drawn towards transforming pain into joy and aliveness. I may sit with the pain for a while, but eventually, it gets transformed into something worth living for. There is something within me that won't allow despair to win. I look at life as experiencing all that comes my way and try to make the best of it without sugar coating what's happening. We all have the choice to challenge and step into ourselves.

When I met Emily, I not only discovered yoga and the transformative impact self-care could have on a soul, but I was also introduced to my reflection, which sent me hurling on a path through self-inquiry toward my true self. I was discovering vocabulary to put to things I knew about myself, but didn't have a reference point for, like being an empath and an intuitive, or being claircognizant and realizing I was a medium. This is what my friend Melissa had "alerted" me to almost thirteen years prior when she called on me to speak her post-mortem message at her own funeral, and what my brother, Tony, had reminded me of that was right under my nose.

In 2012 I discovered Sue Frederick and took her course to become certified as an Intuitive Grief Coach, and the following year, as an Intuitive Life Coach. In 2014 Emily told me about *Giving Spirit Form*, a group circle with a year-long commitment that uses Enneagram, shamanic practices, and inquiry for self-growth. It was, and still is, through this monthly group (which I've attended for seven of the past nine years) that I've come to know the truth of who I am. This group is the reason I can write this book and the impetus for the work I do with others.

These discoveries of my true self coincided with Maria graduating high school. At fifty years old, I was finally figuring out what I was going to be when I grew up! I had finally come into doing what my soul was made for.

My purpose is to be of service in the realm of transformation. I help people become realigned with their souls by guiding them to come home to the truth of who they are. This is an ever-evolving, ever-expanding, and ever-changing dynamic between self, situation, and personality. What I hold close to my heart and share through my voice is a strong sense of self that is grounded in clarity and an understanding that everything is impermanent, and we are all one.

While our physical appearances and the way we animate ourselves may come in many varieties, our essential correspondence has us functioning in accordance with the laws of nature, whether we realize it or not. The common thread is that we all arrive in this world in a similar manner, and we all depart it according to our condition. We arrive with, and leave from, a body. What happens in between has as much variation to it as the number of beings participating in this game, or show, of life. With this knowledge, which stems from a deep inner source that lives within my bones, I've learned to remember that I am here to share this wisdom and to help others, if they choose, to understand their place in this world and live it out in a way that is inherent to them.

My sense of *knowing* has offered me a grounded place to align to, even when I was blind to the fears I was pushing away due to implicit beliefs and conditioned behavior. I chose to make my existence matter by being of service to others, which has always fed a deeper part of me, a part that offers peace to my existence. When I am in contact with this place of peace, I am open to the potential that life offers me. This *knowing*, or strong intuition, has been with me my entire life. It has allowed me to understand our human experience as spiritual. We are spiritual energies encased in our physical bodies – for now.

How we approach life will often reflect back to us in ways that will either hinder or help us navigate more smoothly. It was John O'Donohue who said, "What you encounter, recognize or discover depends to a large degree on the quality of your approach... When we approach with reverence, great things decide to approach us."

We are always the one in our own way. Allowing and recognizing what is occurring in the moment, without attaching stories to it, helps life go more smoothly. However, this is a lifelong journey to navigate, and as a young child without engagement around such questions, I had no choice but to rely on myself.

I thrive in understanding, which brings me clarity. I can listen to *the beyond,* and I can hear the pain of those here in the world. I am a sensitive being, and therefore feel tuned in, but also have to know how and when to tune out if necessary. I love listening. It helps me make sense of life and my surroundings. Clarity can reside within listening. With these deep listening skills, acquired from being a lifelong observer of and witness to others, and through the certified Intuitive Work I completed with Sue Frederick, I have a platform to help people in a way that fulfills my soul, rather than ignore or deplete it. I now put my natural intuitive abilities of empathy, sensitivity, compassion, and resilience to work by helping others achieve what I have – I have discovered my true self, and you can too.

I feel most alive, or at least most in contact with the pulse of life, in the company of life-or-death scenarios. It's as though my soul was made for being between worlds. I've never been afraid of listening to messages or inclinations from beyond. I hear more truth from what I can't see, and find it easier to trust in the unseen than what seems to be appearing right in front of me. I believe it's this ability to listen to and trust in what I can't make logical sense of that allows me to be the spiritual medium I was born to be. I stepped into the call of being an intuitive and spiritual medium when I had a platform, or an acceptable container, to deliver my services to the public. I now had a title to attach to my innate abilities and a reason for being here.

Since 2013 I've helped countless people connect with their departed loved ones who have crossed over. I also help people remember the truth of who they are, because I've contacted the truth of who I am beyond my conditioned self. The easiest way for me to stay connected to this truth is through silencing my mind and being a witness to myself. I've learned that vulnerability and self-compassion are the keys to transformation, and how I may exist among joy and aliveness, while also living among the hardships life brings.

My desire to put my gifts into the world stems from my experience of my own transformation. My superpower, which I believe is listening, is what drove me to put myself out in the world in a way that may be of service to others. It's ironic, though, because my original wounding at the tender young age of four was due to not being listened to. Instead of mimicking the manner in which I was raised, I learned to listen to most everything and everyone around me and became attuned to their energetic vibrations. Some might call this hypervigilance, but I view it as something bigger than me. I can sense the nuance and subtleness of situations and hear beyond the words spoken. I also see the potential of people – often before they do.

When someone is seen for who they are and this is reflected back to them, miracles begin to occur. This was not something I grew up with, and especially not the reflection part, which made it even harder to recognize if another person saw me or not. In order to survive in a way that felt safe to me, I learned to accommodate the needs of others.

I've come to understand that my nervous system was hijacking my perceived idea that if another person's emotional needs were met, and they were taken care of, then so was I. I developed quite the defense system as a result, which prevented me from recognizing the truth of myself, rather, fooling myself into believing I was fine and didn't need anything.

It's easy to not really know oneself deeply if one's needs are not allowed to be part of the equation. I have, however, always had a deep awareness of myself and an understanding of whether or not a situation was safe. I just didn't take to heart the idea that my needs mattered, or that I even had needs. But I always knew what suited my soul. For example, I knew how far to go with risk-taking and where to draw the line before landing in a situation that could be detrimental. I've always had a knowing of right action – meaning what I was doing pushed the envelope just enough, but not further than it should. I could always sense when enough was enough. This knowing I've always had, especially as a child, helped me feel less alone. But my whole structure of self was built around believing my needs didn't matter, and therefore, believing it was normal not to have them.

I can now see my life, and especially the four years prior to meeting Emily, as a constant denial of myself, my voice, and my needs. I muted my voice and pushed my needs down even further in order to help Alanna any way I could. In doing so, I did make her life safe and comfortable enough for her to succeed at what she needed to accomplish at that time in her life. I became a place for her to land softly so she could live out the natural stages of a young teenager. Me being her caregiver, as opposed to someone else, allowed Alanna to not have to think about directing her own care. I knew what to do, and I did it with compassion and attention to detail. This freed up her energy to put towards succeeding at school and having a social life. I tried to help her keep things as "normal" as possible, but without directing some of that compassion into myself, I was inevitably headed towards burnout.

As a way of unconsciously feeling safe, I learned to appease the needs of others before my own. The origin of the word appease is *peace*. I can honestly say now that what I was always looking for, unconsciously, was peace in my life. And I found that by taking care of others. Much of the time I didn't even know what my needs were, or that I even had them, because I was merging with others to feel at peace. This took on many forms, such as being easy-going, going with the flow, acting as though nothing bothered me, not rocking the boat, not speaking up when I felt differently than what was being presented, and allowing the decisions of another to take precedence because it was easier for someone else to make a decision than for me to try and access a part of me that had to determine what I liked or didn't like. I was hiding, ignoring, and not honoring my true self, as though I was numb to my own needs and desires.

The interesting thing about this, however, is that while small decisions were always more difficult for me, big decisions were easier for me to access, especially when there was a decision or crossroads in which the only one who would be affected by the decision was me. In these situations, I can stand up and honor my soul, regardless of the repercussions. I attribute this to still being in alignment with myself – as though my soul has always known when to honor the big things in my life. Despite being out of touch with my voice and my own needs, I could still align with what was important for my soul, such as my imagination, curiosity, and a connection to the more real and more intense aspects of life. When another is affected by my decision, however, it weighs on me a bit more, almost like I don't want to be responsible for the outcome, or that I don't value my own choices the way I value theirs. I assume this is because my voice wasn't valued as a small child.

I've come to learn that my operating process is unconsciously dependent on four significant qualities. There are multiple operating systems in life and ancient teachings we can reference in order to learn more about ourselves, but this one hit home for me in that it speaks to my life story and the qualities that actually calm my nervous system. These qualities are my foundation for harmonious interactions, and I find I actually provide them in my own work with others. I can see that when these qualities are not energetically accessible in my field, something has the potential to go communicatively awry. These qualities are care, trust, connection and engagement.

While I may have not always been able to verbalize or project these foundational qualities for myself because of my own conditioning away from them, I can resonate with the energy they exude and the safety and peace that manifests when they are available, either from myself or with another. I am triggered when my heart is in the right place but I don't receive compassionate care, trust in my actions, a connection with another's heart, or the engagement with them from a clear, present place. Then I have the potential to spin out. The closer I am to the relationship, the more intense the spin can be.

I've done an incredible amount of work to notice these triggers and prevent the resulting emotional pivot before it might get out of hand. I know I must come from a place of directing and embodying these qualities myself first, and not just for myself, but towards others as well. What can anger me and leave me feeling defeated is when I'm not receiving this from someone else because of their own internal blocks. However, the more I can stay in my own lane and acknowledge another for their own perspective, as well as their own internal limitations, I can remain more at peace with myself.

We are interdependent beings and we are affected by others. It takes practice to achieve mindfulness and detach your own behavior from others', and it is certainly not always easy. In fact, it is said that 95% percent of the time we are in our subconscious! A lot of our time is spent not being present, but rather stuck in the past or fretting about the future, all under the guise of believing we are in the present moment. Nuanced and subtle are these qualities, and yet, by becoming a witness and observing my own actions, it is possible to discern who or what is in the driver's seat.

In moments of rage and hysteria (the rare moments I fell into deep despair), I was not available to myself with the care, trust, connection, and engagement I needed to carry on in a way that would serve me on a deep, nourishing level. It wasn't until Emily entered my life that I was genuinely shown these qualities. She saw me at my core and reflected back to me what I'd been missing my entire life – the connection and engagement of a trusting, caring human. She knew first hand of the hardships of being caretaker to a loved one with spinal cord injury. She saw me in my dedication as a mother and my compassion as a caregiver. She saw me, and that allowed me to begin to see myself. She offered me the unspoken permission to trust that the things I knew to be true for myself, my deep self, were in fact valid, and that I could rest easy knowing another saw the world like I did.

The possibilities and expansion of one's soul, and therefore human expression, are wholly attainable when an honest connection occurs with oneself and with another. This connection can enable a soul to witness truth. I realized this was not just a fantasy I was playing out in my own internal world, but a reality that others could recognize, want access to, and experience for themselves. I was coming alive in the remembrance of who I am, and I was rising into my soul's purpose to help others do the same.

It took me a good year to put all these moving parts of what was transforming inside of me together. This was a time I relished in the spark of awe and amazement that shedding layers of myself could unearth. It also allowed some space and breathing room to arise between Alanna, myself, and our enmeshed lives. While Alanna's injury brought, and still brings, moments of struggle for her, and for me as a witness to her, we have, for the most part, navigated through it with grace.

Focusing inward and discovering a new awareness of myself allowed me to breathe easier in my role meeting Alanna's needs. I was, for the first time, honoring my own needs as I continued to uncover them, which gave us both more freedom. While I am still Alanna's primary care provider, she has respected my Soul Work and supported my endeavor to simultaneously create a life for myself out of desire and spiritual purpose while continuing to care for her needs. We could then relate to one another in a new way as we both set out to develop our passions and put our work out into the world. She focused on event planning, which eventually led to her obtaining a certification in Functional Nutrition. I became an Intuitive Coach and answered my calling to work as a medium.

Maria graduated high school the year I began pursuing my own career as an Intuitive Coach. She has shared with me that she learned to trust her intuition more because of my work, not only through witnessing me in my endeavors, but also in being a recipient of my work. She was on the "normal" track of going off to college and beginning her independence. Unlike Alanna, who went to college but lived at home. Maria's time away allowed her to learn how to depend solely on herself, although she already had a taste of it at home, especially as a young girl, when Alanna and I lived in a hospital for four months. Whether or not I was physically home with her, my emotional attunement to her needs gave her a secure foundation to learn how to take care of herself, which she had to, and she did beautifully. She spent her junior year of college in Sweden, traveling solo to fifteen different countries. Her independence, and her ability to set personal boundaries, has put me in awe of her. I can only imagine she saw in me what NOT to do – forget thyself and forgo thy needs.

I am beyond proud of both my daughters for their ability to persevere and continually question themselves of what is important for them to thrive in their own lives. They learn through trial and error, but they don't pigeonhole themselves if they run into a setback. I'd like to think that watching their mother strive for what is important to her, beyond my roles as a mother and caregiver, has helped them to unapologetically strive for what is inherently important to them. This is revolutionary to me, as my time raising my children, which I loved and chose to do, was approached from the perspective of giving up myself for them.

My mother would often tell me during the days of having young children to *find something of my own*. I tried, and I dabbled, but I really had no sense of what that could possibly be. Just before getting pregnant with Alanna, and on and off after having Maria, I did teach swim lessons to young children. Other than that, nothing landed for me the way Soul Work has in making me feel alive and true to myself. That feeling is how I know it is my purpose to share it.

We are spiritual beings having a human experience. The challenge for me, as well as the joy in knowing it exists, is the idea of having a choice at any given moment, that regardless of how hard life can be – and living with a spinal cord injury is undeniably difficult – the choice to find grace amongst hardship is possible. This choice allows for resilience, growth, and potential to continue when all else feels lost and hopeless.

It is not in my blood to allow the hardest aspects of life to get the upper hand. They are my teachers and my guiding lights to continue striving for the beauty and opportunity that resilience can bring being a mother, wife, caregiver, entrepreneur, writer, daughter, sister, a dog mama, and a friend. And it is a *practice*.

Knowing oneself truthfully and compassionately enough to consciously make choices in the face of hardship, and living within that potential, is the foundation to practicing Soul Work. One of the most exciting aspects of this adventure is that the discovery of self never ends. It only becomes more fulfilling.

PART 2

❖

THE ELEMENTS OF SOUL WORK

HINDSIGHT

Together we fell into
What we never could have imagined ~ restrictions,
quarantines, loss, death.
Everything we had known before was pulled out from
under us.
No one way seems to work.
Those who comply and those who deny.
You can't really ever know why.

The thing is, though,
What has been called upon us as a people, is to
Engage in a way of life
Not seen before our time.
These are moments of extraordinary shifts, how will
You be defined as time unravels?

~Angela DeSalvo

CHAPTER 8

PRACTICE: SOUL WORK

"...we can only be said to be alive in those moments
when our hearts are conscious of our treasure..."

Thornton Wilder, *The Woman of Andros*

What is Soul Work?

I refer to Soul Work as the work I do. It's about getting to
the core of our issues and beneath the personality to understand
what drives us in our behavior. Our soul will always bring us back
to our truth if we listen. When we can recognize our essence,
or our unconditioned being, we are in resonance with our soul.
We are animated by our soul, and at the same time, we can be
inhibited by our personality and the conditioned aspects of our
existence. Soul Work is the truth that lies below the familiar. It
is what lingers in the unknown aspects of ourselves and opens us
up to our true nature. It takes connecting to trust, vulnerability,
courage, and compassion to begin to access this part of ourselves.

Soul work is the ability to listen to the soft, quiet message
inside of us, whether it be a voice, a sensation, a feeling, or a
knowing. I love this work because I love discovering the root

of mine and others' internal conflicts. I find this sheds weight to reveal yet another layer of a person's full expression. I believe this is our birthright, to express fully as the human beings that we are, being guided by our spirits and pursuant to our soul's purpose. The discernment comes from knowing what is merely the personality, versus what is one's true nature, and then being at choice of how to navigate through the former into the latter.

Soul work takes you on a journey through an intimate perspective. Taking on an intimate perspective is conceptual in nature and liberating in practice. The elements of practicing Soul Work include connection, self-care, reflection, acceptance, presence, practice, and sacred space. When an individual pursues Soul Work wholeheartedly, they begin exercising these elements like different muscles of the body, becoming stronger and more adept in themselves as they continue the practice.

Soul Work is a process guided by my deep listening skills, combined with a set of tools that can provide you with a better understanding of human behavior – specifically your own. These tools range from Enneagram and numerology to astrology, as well as having a basic understanding of the nervous system and psychology, such as with attachment theory, the impacts of trauma, and mental dis-ease.

The magic that occurs, in time, from Soul Work is a closer relationship with one's true nature. This can be fleeting, as we are mercurial beings. However, when one experiences their true self for the first time, it is not a feeling that is forgotten. It can be hard to hold on to continually, which is why practicing Soul Work is so important. Soul work does not require perfection, only participation. This work heals us, and it keeps us connected to something bigger than ourselves.

CHAPTER 9

ELEMENTS OF SOUL WORK: CONNECTION

Connection

To make a connection is to make contact. Connection is establishing successful communication and relating to, or being in harmony with, another person. Connection is the first element of Soul Work, because without it there is no contact, and without contact, there is no sense of the present moment or a soul's truth in it. In Soul Work, making a connection requires Trust, Vulnerability, Courage, and Compassion.

Connection can be elusive, which is why Soul Work is so important. Connecting with a spiritual guide or coach (such as myself) in the initial stages of Soul Work lays the foundation for trust and safety. What transpires from there is the capacity to become vulnerable and discover how the "familiar" sense of connecting to oneself may be the very thing getting in the way of feeling at ease in your body, thoughts, and feelings.

For most of my life, the familiar way I showed up for myself was to feel a tremendous sense of responsibility to those closest to me or whom I care about deeply. This was not a conscious feeling – more of an autopilot reaction to how I made myself available to others, my perception of their needs, and whether or not they asked me for help. I only became aware I was acting on autopilot once I became intimately involved and connected to myself, and I allowed vulnerability to bring my unconscious, internal pains to the surface.

Connection is what propelled me to set forth and continue on my inner journey. Having always been a spiritual and curious individual, my connection to myself has never wavered. The difference, however, was when I learned to trust myself to be vulnerable in that connection. This was made easier in a safe space of non-judgmental witnesses. My safe space was a facilitated circle called *Giving Spirit Form*. Attending this circle gave me the courage to show up for myself in a way that required me to be honest with my emotions and make room for self-compassion, as well as fuel the compassion I already had for the human plight of others (the human condition).

As a person who dominates in the structure of a five in the Enneagram, connection can often feel foreign. In fact, within this particular structure, it feels safer to isolate and be very selective with who gets access to me. This was true for most of my life, mostly unconsciously, as is the case with all of our Enneagram structures. However, once I was able to make an honest, vulnerable connection with myself, I yearned for connection with others. It was a lack of deep connection with others that had kept me from myself for so long.

The safety and honesty established through connection in Soul Work allows for trust, vulnerability, courage, and compassion to arise. Through my journey of embracing the elements of Soul Work and utilizing the tools that encourage an intimate perspective, I discovered the very thing that kept me from myself was the very thing I needed to catapult me into my truest self. This is how I remembered the Truth of Who I Am.

Connecting with Trust

In Soul Work, trust is the ability to have faith in the unknown, and to also have the confidence to be curious with what sensations in the body, memories arising in the mind, and thoughts coming into the present moment are trying to reveal. Trust is essential in the context of Soul Work, because it helps to inform you of what is just below the surface of the familiar aspects of your personality. I've found it helps to trust that all is working in divine order for this process to be successful, and time and time again, when I lean into trusting in the process of life, things go smoothly.

Having trust is being able to sit with the stillness and rest assured it's ok to not know everything. Having trust is being able to sense the nuances and subtle shifts that occur in life when the soul is revealing a part of itself. I continue to relearn how to do this as I deconstruct my Enneagram structure throughout my own Soul Work journey, which is a lifelong pursuit and practice.

Relaxing into the unknown is an act of feminine energy. That's not a reference to gender, but to an energy within each of us that can be tapped into, no matter our sex.

Anxiety is the resistance to trusting.

Calmness, or groundedness, is a sign that trust has been added to the Soul Work equation. When I trust in the process of life, and when I sidestep my desire to be in the know, instead trusting the unknown to reveal what is trying to surface, I can move forward with less suffering or worry.

For example, writing this book was a direct product of connection and trust, both within myself and with others, from the Soul Work I've done and continue to do. Once I found the right guide, in terms of a coach and an editor, I was able to trust the process of creation and completion and find the right momentum forward. Prior to this guidance, I was writing without structure or real direction.

Guidance is crucial on any path, and this guidance can also come in the form of trust. This connection to trust must be cultivated from within, and in most cases, requires at least one person to witness the work being done. When two or more people are gathered in sacred intention, and trusting one another together in the process of Soul Work, miracles can occur. What better time than now to begin getting curious?

Curiosity will always lead you to a place beyond where you are now. The trick is to trust where you are guided.

Connecting with Vulnerability

The Latin origin of the word *vulnerable* relates to wounding or injury. To be vulnerable in Soul Work is to expose oneself to core wounds or emotional traumas. It's a willingness to connect with, trust in and express painful emotions, which are oftentimes perceived as weaknesses because they subconsciously relate to childhood wounding. This is where we begin to push down and turn away from ourselves, because we were turned away by a caregiver in a moment when we needed to be comforted in our pain.

I've experienced extreme vulnerability, and I know it's possible to come out the other side stronger and more closely connected to yourself. In one particular instance, during a check-in for the circle I participate in, in which each group member gives a brief introductory monologue expressing what is currently arising in their life, I was severely impacted by the check-in of others. What transpired was a very vulnerable act arising from a feeling of safety, trust, and connection. I began to feel so much emotional pain in my body that had never been processed or acknowledged before, but I allowed the crying and shaking to move through me, which helped me wash away years of denying myself access to deeper parts of me.

A friend mentioned to me later that she had no idea I carried so much emotion inside of me. We both attended this particular circle and carpooled to it together. It threw her for a loop to share free-flowing, upbeat conversations with me on the drive and then witness the emergence of all this pain coming through me in the circle. I explained to her that I was just as much in the dark about the buried pain inside of me as she was, because it hadn't made its way into our conversations. This is how subtle and disassociated we can be from our own pain, and the way this can manifest for many of us is to disconnect emotionally from ourselves.

There will never be a "one-way ticket" or magical cure for someone to fix what feels broken within them. The point is to be open to what arises along the winding path towards healing. If I hadn't allowed myself to be affected by others' check-ins, or felt safe enough to express my emotions, then I most likely would have played the familiar game of shoving my needs, voice, and feelings downward, and stay in front of passively listening while remaining disassociated from myself.

If I hadn't allowed myself to be vulnerable, I wouldn't have allowed myself to be emotionally impacted – because that would indicate that I have needs. Living with this idea of not having needs kept me at a safe distance from myself. However, I was given the choice to be vulnerable because I felt safe while connected to a circle of trust, and thus was able to break through these implicit belief patterns. This helped me change my conditioned behaviors and introduce a feeling of liberation in my life, which ultimately brought me closer to myself.

I am now thriving in the truth of Who I Am, versus surviving in the familiar aspects of who I thought I was.

Liberation emanates from the ability to come face-to-face with our not-so-pretty or too-easily felt emotions. The shame, fear, anxiety, anger, and guilt that keep us from accessing the truth behind these feelings subside once they are allowed to exist, and be expressed, in real time. Like Mr. Rogers said, "If it's mentionable, it's manageable." In Soul Work, I offer my clients a safe space to be held, seen, and vulnerable. This foundation of trust allows the mentioning to become more manageable.

Connecting with Courage

The origin of the word *courage* denotes the heart as the seat of feelings. Having courage is having strength in the face of pain or grief. Many people turn away from pain or grief out of fear. This is especially true in Western cultures, which tend to put the highest value on overworking and monetary success, thus people are not as readily nurtured in a way that values our humanness and the inevitable pain and grief that arises from living. Working hard and earning money are not inherently bad qualities, but the excessive praise and prioritized attention given for overworking and becoming ultra rich leaves little room to express the pain and grief that may arise as a result of working too hard and managing money.

We saw on the world stage how Simone Biles, a hard-working gymnast (and I'd imagine wealthy individual), had the courage to announce she was stepping down from the Olympic finals for the sake of preserving the health of her mind and body, which are both crucially important for her work to be successful. The world was stunned with her courage to make this decision, and it wasn't all positive. In fact, it startled the media so much at first that they were unsure of how to report it. My point is that this culture does not naturally value courage when it comes to addressing, or even acknowledging, pain or grief.

In Soul Work, it takes courage to simply show up for oneself, as saying "yes" to yourself, possibly for the first time, has the potential to bring up pain and grief and create many new sensations in the body, as well as new ways of thinking. Without courage, the tendency is to emotionally spin out in the face of memories that are old and familiar. With courage, a foundation is laid for truth to arise without letting fear stop it in its tracks. My mentor once said, "Truth naturally arises when the heart is open."

If courage originates in the heart, then the work has already begun when an individual shows up for oneself with the intention of discovering that which is not yet known, that which resides deep within their soul's core. Because the act of showing up for oneself can be subtle, elusive, and not always seen for what it actually is, Soul Work requires courage to overcome the tendency to delay or stay stuck in the familiar. This is multifaceted because habits die hard and the familiar is comforting – we are always the one in our own way. For this reason, a spiritual mentor, guide, or coach who can offer a different perspective can help open the window of tolerance for a person to see life in a new way, especially as it might relate to their conditioned habits and unconscious patterns that were established very early in life.

Courage is the first element necessary in any work that involves looking within oneself. For the person who walks the path of personal exploration, courage is already at the helm. Courage paves the way for everything else to begin to surface. It's important to recognize courage within oneself and the groundwork it lays for further exploration. In doing so, it becomes easier to be vulnerable and trust in the process.

I think of courage like a friend. I see it as an opportunity to face that which I am being led to with strength as a companion, especially when I'm in the dark as to why. While I'm quick to understand if a situation is not in my best interest, my curiosity can get the best of me when I sense that the lesson at hand may enhance my potential, and it takes courageous discernment to respond and act in the best way possible.

Connecting with Compassion

Compassion is the extension of warmth and care when confronted with someone else's or one's own suffering. Compassion is the precursor to empathy. Active compassion is the desire to alleviate and prevent another's suffering, and an act of compassion is defined by its helpfulness. The qualities of compassion are patience, wisdom, kindness, perseverance, warmth, and resolve.

In Soul Work, compassion is extending this warmth as feelings of old limiting beliefs arise. The process of connecting to one's truth is likely to produce some form of suffering within oneself, but with compassion, it can unfold in a way that's empowering and life-giving, as opposed to disheartening and diminishing of life-force.

Without compassion, suffering can become a way of life, because it can easily be contacted. Suffering is familiar, and serves as a point of contact for a person to believe *this is just who I am*. It is worth asking who you would be if you weren't who you thought you were based on habitual behavior, because you can then begin to see who you are as a person *in flow,* expressing yourself as a reflection of your true essence, not your condition. To do this successfully, you need compassion from a guiding witness, as well as the self-compassion to express your truth without inhibition.

When we can offer ourselves compassion, we can truly begin to heal as we realize that suffering is a choice. When we extend compassion to ourselves, we are allowed to be less than perfect, a condition many of us unconsciously place upon ourselves. It may manifest in self-sabotage, or not feeling good enough or worthy of trying, especially in areas we feel vulnerable in. With self-compassion, we can breathe a little easier.

In the years of being witnessed in a safe space as my deepest, darkest pains were revealed – pains I had no idea I was even suppressing – I was met with the grace of self-compassion. I allowed myself to feel what had been buried deep inside. In time, I was able to forgive any perceived wrongdoing from another, as well as forgive myself for the results of the limiting beliefs I'd armored around myself for protection. I saw the vulnerability of the human condition, and I allowed myself and others the compassion to live within the complexity of it all.

CHAPTER 10

ELEMENTS OF SOUL WORK: SELF-CARE

Self-Care

Taking care of yourself is making your own needs a priority. Soul Work is the pillar of self-care because it is the driving force behind aligning you with your higher self, thus unveiling what your soul needs in order to be authentically expressed. This alignment makes life easier to navigate with clarity and an understanding of yourself and others.

The starting point of transformative self-care is becoming the *inner witness*, and beginning to notice and bring awareness to, without judgment, your patterns and habits of behavior. This is what was significantly life-changing for me in the work I began a decade ago. I became a non-judgmental witness to my own behavior, which nourished an awareness of my true self that I hadn't experienced before.

This can be an especially hard task if you're conditioned to deny your own needs, and you believe taking care of others is more important than taking care of yourself. To serve others is important, but when it's done at the expense of forgetting yourself, or with the unconscious motive that you'll get something in return, like similar treatment or a false feeling of self-care, you're hijacking the perceived feeling of others as your own. Depletion or resentment are likely to be the outcome, thus caring for others in order to care for yourself becomes futile. In order to truly take care of yourself, you must ask *what do I need?*

Caring for the Mind

The mind remembers and the mind thinks. The mind harbors, catalogs, and processes our memories and thoughts, but the mind can also betray us. Our *hardware* is set up in childhood. We then go into the world rarely updating our *programs*, which is why we act by conditions, or with a *virus* in our system. An uncared-for mind creates illusions from the persona, or from the shadow self, which can then cause you to function on autopilot, remembering and thinking in the familiar mental state of surviving trauma. Trauma is anything that happens that is too much, too fast, or too soon, which leaves you unable to process what has occurred. It can be major trauma like physical or sexual abuse, or it can be a *small "t" trauma*, as in my case.

As a four-year-old, not being acknowledged by my mother in my crying and screaming for the boys to leave while I dressed, didn't offer me what I needed. I needed my voice to be heard and a boundary for my privacy to be established in order for me to know that everything was ok and I was safe. I was left to my own accord as a developing child in a situation that, in my perception, was threatening. My coping strategy became denying my own needs and tending to others so I wouldn't feel totally forgotten.

We are intelligent beings with an ability to cope with what we don't receive in order to still receive what we innately desire, which is to feel safe and loved. My way of coping was to unconsciously try to control my surroundings by assuming others perceived situations as I did, which in turn made me feel less vulnerable or prone to emotional abandonment.

In Soul Work, taking care of the mind is a practice in actively adapting to your internal world in order to feel safe in the present moment. Cues from our nervous system can inform us why we are thinking as we do in certain situations. Awareness of these cues give us the opportunity to stop in the moment and readjust our thinking.

An example would be hearing ambulance sirens and immediately feeling threatened or scared. You may think the worst is going to happen, because in the past, this was connected to a direct experience. Personally, I get a burning or pulling sensation on my shoulder blades. I've come to realize my mind has just latched onto fear in response to certain situational or sensational cues.

While this can be extremely subtle, when I stop long enough to inquire within, I realize I am anticipating something in the future. When this occurs, it is usually a thought about a presumed outcome for something that hasn't happened – it's all in my mind. I've become skilled at noticing the physical signs in my body that prompt a mental response, and take it as an opportunity to check in within myself to see what the sensation is actually telling me. Once I make contact with the reality of what's happening, and I tell myself there is nothing to worry about or to fear, the sensation in my shoulders subsides and my mind settles.

The mind is properly cared for by allowing and noticing when it is in the present moment. This is when clarity becomes the driver – with our perception as the compass. The beauty of Soul Work is it teaches us that our mind is best used for discernment.

Most of us are used to our minds telling ourselves stories, and worse yet, believing all of them. Just because we think a thought does not make it true, nor do we have to believe it. Discernment allows us to discover the truth of the matter, and the reality of what is. When we can be honest with what we're feeling around our thoughts, we can begin to discern the microscopic truths of what's being presented. We can drop the defenses around a particular thought or belief and allow truth to arise.

My core wound kept me from my true nature for much of my life, until I learned how to see and listen to the truth of who I am. I began to remember that I matter, simply because I exist, and that I didn't have to make someone else matter more than me in order to give myself a sense of existing. The need to grasp or chase my unconscious and familiar belief that, "My needs don't matter, but I'll make sure yours do," fell away in time.

Self-care of the mind is affirmation that the self, matters, and that one's true self is worth remembering and knowing. Self-care of the mind is bringing attention to the inner witness, and becoming aware of past memories and current thought processes without judgment. This itself is a practice and comes about by being able to witness our thoughts as an observer of them, not as an active participant of creating them. This process unlocks self-compassion. An uncared-for mind bears the weight of the nervous system's reaction to emotional injury, thus thinks in a conditioned manner, while the cared for mind unlocks the liberation of expressing true self.

Because of Soul Work, I am now skilled at understanding my own mind and being able to discern when a story from my past is hijacking my perception of the current moment. Habits die hard, however, so this takes practice and a conscious awareness of oneself to begin to cultivate. Empowering the mind to be in control, but not the master, requires someone to be aligned, or integrated, with their true self.

Caring for the mind allows us to rewrite our memories with authenticity as the author, and therefore, think with clarity within the present moment. It allows for our adult-self to make the decisions, instead of acting from the programming of the child-self, or from when the initial trauma took place and our minds were not capable of choosing how to move forward. Coming into our adult-self, and thus tapping into the potential of our adult minds, creates choice.

Caring for the Body

As spiritual beings having a human experience, our spirits are housed in our bodies. The body gives the spirit form and houses the memories of our experiences in our nervous system. The body remembers, and it takes rewiring the nervous system to ultimately release the outdated stories that no longer serve the situation.

It's important to incorporate, move, and use our bodies in any capacity we can, otherwise we rely on our minds too much. Our mind can take us anywhere. The body, however, can only exist in the present moment, which is why it's important to care for it, and useful to connect with it.

We can do this by activating our five senses – sight, sound, taste, touch and smell – or by activating our memories stored in the brain that trigger our nervous system, and sitting with the sensations that arise as a result. These sensations may feel heavy in the extremities, or be more targeted, as with contractions or pressure in the torso area. It could feel like a block, or an opening in the heart or a tightness around the throat. Tightness in the throat region is often associated with a fear of speaking.

A few years back, I experienced an uncomfortable sensation in my throat for a couple of weeks that I intuitively knew wasn't health related, as in acid reflux or a cold. I was divinely led to a shamanic practitioner. During my session with her, where she was in an altered state and journeying on my behalf (similar to the meditation I do on behalf of my clients), she discovered an aspect of me from another lifetime. I was tied up in the corner of an old, barn-like structure. She intuited it as me being burned at the stake for speaking my truth. I hadn't told her of the sensation in my throat, but her description corresponded to the feeling as a fear of speaking. Needless to say, once I saw her, the annoyance in my throat went away. The fear of speaking – based in my subconscious, limiting belief that I wasn't allowed to – has crept into my life in more ways than one. My own work has offered me the tools to recognize this feeling sooner, and to choose to thank it for showing up, but disregard it as it is not true. I can move beyond the fear.

Caring for and listening to our bodies can enlighten us. When I began doing yoga on a regular basis, a whole new world opened up for me, one that requested I become aware of what was transpiring within me. Movement that can transform us requires the conscious use of our breath. Whenever we are conscious of what we are doing, we land in the present moment with ease and become aware of each inhale and exhale. Breathing is the key to unlocking stored emotions and memories. Deep, slow breathing with long exhales offers a world of difference in the ability to align with ourselves. Breath work allows us to reset in the present moment. Conscious breathing enables us to express reality rather than act hastily upon implicit beliefs. This, too, is a practice.

In Soul Work it's important to become skilled at noticing how your body communicates with you. The body is always trying to provide us information, whereas the mind, if not discerning, is most often creating a story around a triggering sensation. This disconnect from ourselves can cause us to leave the present moment and spin into fear, anxiety, or depression. With time, practice, self-compassion, and the vulnerability to become curious (instead of resistant) to why these sensations are occurring, a person's mind can trace back to a time when the body didn't feel safe.

This is my story. In my inner work, I've been able to understand the origin of my fear of speaking when it came to addressing my own needs or speaking my truth. When I began taking care of my body, and took note of the physical sensations my memories stirred up, I could then release the story around them and embrace my truth, rather than remain stuck in the familiar.

Memories stored in the body can make us feel as though we're experiencing them in real time when we get triggered, unless we're consciously aware of them and able to discern the past from the present. This experience of mind-body awareness can either be pleasing or very disruptive to our current state. For example, a memory may be stimulated by the scent of freshly baked cookies and take you back to your childhood. The body then has the opportunity to relax into the present moment with either a pleasing memory from the past, or a traumatic one. Perhaps the smell of cookies brings up a negative sensation in the body, causing the mind to react to a story, such as being scolded for taking a cookie without asking.

When we only engage the mind and forgo the body as a messenger of truth, we use what we perceive as the intelligence of the mind to falsely conceptualize scenarios and believe we are who we think we are based on a story from the past. On the other hand, when we consciously bring our bodies along for the ride instead of neglecting their function, we give ourselves the opportunity to engage in a deeper sense of self, enter the present moment, and turn autopilot off.

Caring for the Heart

Aside from keeping us alive, the purpose of the heart-space is to receive. We receive the heart's daily gift of life, but we don't often recognize or allow ourselves to receive our worth, let alone the good intentions of another. It's often much easier to give, as to receive requires a softness towards oneself, an allowance of what is, and the realization that we matter enough to be given to, which is very different than *taking from*.

It's my belief that at our unconditioned core, we are all born with a soft heart capable of giving and receiving, but through our personal experiences, and the array of trauma that can occur from the human condition, a heart can get closed off and hardened, often without us realizing. When I was mirrored in my expression of giving and began to realize that my needs indeed mattered, I then was able to receive as well as give, not just from myself, but from others.

The familiar coping mechanisms we develop to simply survive as children can get in the way of our hearts, as well as the manner in which we give or receive as adults. Part of surviving is to defend ourselves out of fear. Therefore, in a survival situation, the heart is in no place to receive or give, as both actions can feel very risky. Defense mechanisms are a manifestation of the hardware, so to speak, that was laid out in childhood, most likely at the moment of trauma. If the trauma was repetitive, or never given space to be acknowledged, participating in life can feel like a constant state of risk.

The result is an existence that functions on autopilot. This leaves you cut off from living in the world, but also from yourself, living as though you are of the world, or trapped in the conditional behaviors of your personality. This can feel like being in a cage, unable to see the keys to unlock the bars hanging right in front of you, as though the cage and the self are one in the same.

When your heart is open because it's been softened by the mind's discernment of what's real and the body's present sensations, you can be on the receiving end of joy, potential, and grace. The mind becomes quiet and clear, the body sits grounded and right here, and the heart beats for an authentic life. This is the experience of love, which is what we are all inherently made of. When the mind, body, and heart are integrated and properly taken care of, we can experience peace. This too, like all the elements of Soul Work, is an ongoing practice, because just like in nature, there is always a hidden layer of self just waiting to blossom when the time is right.

Soul Work offers you the opportunity to know what it is to have an open heart.

CHAPTER 11

ELEMENTS OF SOUL WORK: REFLECTION

The Reflection and Remembrance of Self

Taking an intimate perspective requires us to reflect on the experiences that conditioned us and remember the truth of who we are outside of those conditions. While going forward is always recommended, reflection is necessary to gain access to remembrance. When society doesn't reflect on history, the same detrimental outcomes can occur in the future. It's not hard to look at today's society and see where historical reflection, and its subsequent lessons, are not being embraced.

This disregard to learn from the past also sends a message to people at large that remembering the past isn't necessary, enjoyable, nor purposeful. It is instead implied that denial is the best way to approach life. This is the collective trauma humanity faces from widespread implicit beliefs and conditioned behavior. There are pockets of people trying to do the right thing by teaching the value of the sacredness of life, but the systemic mindset is a constant challenge to wade through. It is not modeled for us in our Western society to take accountability for our actions or to offer grace and understanding to others for theirs.

For many, coping with denial is suitable and familiar and they don't feel it necessary to change. This lends itself to coping through self-medication in order to remain in a comfortable state of denial. Our capitalistic, Western society thrives on selling the idea of *Wine Wednesdays* and *Margarita Mondays*, or a pill for just about every human malady. I'm not saying it's a crime to enjoy and partake in libations, or to take necessary medications when called for. However, it does require the ability to make a conscious choice in drawing the line between coping and enjoyment when using addictive substances or partaking in addictive behaviors, whether it be food, drugs, work, sex, fame, or even isolation.

Coping with denial, rather than reflecting and facing the truth, usually requires something to help push down the pain. There are of course benefits to a prescribed medication establishing balance in one's chemistry, but there is a fine line to straddle between personal empowerment and external suggestions which numb the pain, encourage coexistence with denial, and cause you to forgo taking an intimate perspective. Let's face it, reflecting on the past can be difficult and is sure to bring up memories you may not desire to revisit.

Reflection may remind you of a time you were without the necessary tools to know what the next best step could have been, and for that, shame can arise. Or if you weren't satisfied with your behavior towards another or yourself, reflecting upon it may remind you that you should have taken responsibility for your actions when they occurred. Shame, guilt, fear, anxiety, and anger can arise if we look at ourselves with contempt for our behavior, instead of compassion, which is often the case if the other elements of Soul Work are not involved.

Why? Because the overall message from our society does not readily acknowledge pain or grief as valid emotions to reflect upon, therefore we're all affected one way or another by the subtleties of collective denial. It's a sickness that we are so intertwined with in our world that it goes without recognition, instead, all too often diagnosed as an illness or disorder. In reality, it's the oppression of emotions without an outlet for understanding.

For many, living in a constant state of denial is perpetually exhausting and painful. Soul Work is for those who seek transformation, healing, and a choice in the matter, and who are willing to look at themselves from an intimate perspective to remember the truth of who they are, to find it.

Understanding the behaviors of ourselves and others will likely create a lot less angst and frustration among people, opening the door for more clear and compassionate communication. This takes work, though. It requires intention, desire, and a willingness to listen from a place of presence and non-judgment. It requires us to discern the motivation that lies beneath our reactions, beyond our biased, black-and-white thinking, and into an understanding of microscopic, subconscious behavior.

When our reflections and reality can coexist, we are capable of recognizing the truth of ourselves. This is also an ideal. People are complex beings, and if we were taught as children, and especially by society as a whole, that being alive in a human body is a sacred act, and the actions of people as a whole reflected that, then reflecting on the past wouldn't be so hard. It wouldn't be as necessary either, because people would be more conscious of their actions and more present to reality as it's happening.

My journey of reflecting on my past, and offering myself compassion in the process, has empowered me to use my voice unapologetically while advocating for my needs and expressing myself from my soul. I had to reflect on my past in order to remember this is my birthright. It is my right to allow the truth of who I am to be revealed.

It is my hope, my wish, and my vision for humanity for people to commit to their own healing, to want to get along with understanding rather than being right, and to raise children from a place of presence that values and recognizes the uniqueness of each person. There would be no need to reflect on the past if our actions in the present more closely reflected each person's true nature. While this would be a Utopian ideal, remembering who you are at your core is part of the human journey, and seeking the sacredness in life is worth it, in my perspective. It is worth it to reflect on the past and learn to embrace it in all its forms and foibles so remembering the truth isn't so frightening.

We must leave our judgments of the past at the door and learn to embrace grace for the human condition. Remembrance of who you are, and of who we are as spiritual beings, and the realization that who you are at your core is love, leads to liberation from all that makes you beholden to conditions, labels, circumstances or judgements. You don't become less of who you are by reflecting on and remembering the past – you free yourself from who you thought you were, and embrace all that you came here to be.

Through the practice of Soul Work, and with an intimate perspective, you will receive the opportunity to express yourself as the person you were born to be ~ your birthright, as it were.

CHAPTER 12

ELEMENTS OF SOUL WORK: ACCEPTANCE AND ALLOWANCE

An Intimate Perspective

To accept is to receive or permit something either concrete, abstract, or elusive in nature. Furthermore, to be open to whatever it is you are accepting is an act of allowance that requires trust in the unknown, or in the process of life. When we can be mindful enough to get out of our own way, and set aside the patterns and habits we cling to so fiercely, it's easier to trust in the process of life and allow what needs to arise in order to inform us of the decisions we should be making at any given moment. It is possible to be calm in the middle of chaos. It takes practice and trust, as well as an acceptance of the past, the now, and of what the future holds, to allow what is occurring to occur, so we can discern reality from the familiar and understand what is subtly being revealed to us.

The longer I live and recognize the specific times I didn't accept what was happening because I was acting in old, familiar beliefs, I can see that I wasn't as effective, present or content as I could have been in a situation. Growing up with a continuation of crises happening in my family – from mental hospitals to cancer wards – along with a voice I learned was not meant for being heard and my actions becoming dependent on caring for others, I was conditioned to let the familiar run the show and pilot how I responded. When I fall back into this familiar mindset, I can initially feel panicked because perhaps I don't understand what is occurring, and the health of a loved one is threatened by uncertainty. This can be very overwhelming to me.

This overwhelm, I now understand, is comparable to the overwhelm I felt as a four-year-old when my perception of safety was threatened, and I felt uncertain in the moment and in need of the reassurance I didn't receive. That initial trauma manifested into the microscopic subtlety that would continue to dominate how I perceived uncertainty when it came to the health of those near and dear to me.

Before Soul Work, I would check out and disassociate from my emotions, but call upon my actions to try and tend to the needs of others. This was the case when I was alerted to my daughter's injury. I remember feeling myself drop backwards. My husband ran to her with a valid understanding of what had happened. I, on the other hand, approached her with caution and hesitation because I didn't understand the reality of what was occurring. But as her mother, I did comfort her with love and presence as I looked her in the eyes and held space for her fear and mine, in silence.

I remember thinking on the drive to the hospital if we'd just heeded our own intuition – from Doug's gut feeling not to go on the trip, to the voice I ignored in my head telling me to ask the cab to come back for us at 10pm – this wouldn't have happened. But it did. While logically playing the *what-if* game had me connecting the dots towards Alanna's accident never occurring, ("If I'd just listened to the signs!"), accepting what happened is what allowed us to move forward together.

Surrending to divine order is a necessary step in acceptance.

As the years have passed since Alanna's injury, and after being her primary caregiver all this time, I've learned a lot about accepting what has occurred and allowing what is occurring to come forward. I've found there's nothing quite like landing in the present moment when you're required to be available to the physical needs of another, as in the case of paralysis, and accepting it is the only way to actually move forward.

Acceptance of what *has* happened in the past, what *is* happening in the present, and what *will* happen in the future can be a delicate state of affairs. The mind may believe accepting something completely means nothing will change, but acceptance has to be at the forefront of thought and action for progress to be made and momentum to occur. I finally realized this when the anger I housed over my daughter's injury did nothing but drain me. An aspect of reality was being ignored and stagnation crept in, especially in how I cared for my soul.

Change is the only constant in life. Being in alignment with what is occurring gives way to allowing what is in the moment to occur without fighting it or creating familiar stories from it. In the long run, acceptance and allowance keep us in the present moment and make space for us to show up authentically – not as our conditioned selves. This is not an easy way to live all the time because we are habitual creatures, and the behaviors of the conditioned self are very subtle. However, with continual practice, Soul Work enables us to recognize our conditioned ways, and if interested, align with our authentic selves. This is how we learn to thrive in life, instead of merely surviving in the only way we've learned how- with implicit beliefs and through conditioning. You can accept the past, allow the present, and move forward into the future with joy and potential joining you for the ride.

CHAPTER 13

ELEMENTS OF SOUL WORK: PRESENCE

An estimated 95% of the human brain's activity occurs unconsciously, meaning the vast majority of the decisions we make, actions we take, our emotions, and our behaviors reside beyond our conscious awareness – in the subconscious. This is an astoundingly high percentage of time we spend in a state of subconscious cognition, and yet we can accomplish so much in our lives. It's no wonder, then, that acting on autopilot comes so naturally to us. Autopilot, or behaving and thinking in a familiar, conditioned manner, is our brain's default setting. This is a survival mechanism, which is discussed in further detail in the next chapter.

The cultivation of presence, or mindfulness, doesn't come naturally. It takes a persistent level of conscious work to achieve and integrate into our daily lives. Meditation is a well-known technique to welcome in presence, but there are also little things you can do to feel more present as you proceed with your day-to-day activities, such as noticing objects in your current surroundings, touching things as you name them to make contact with the current moment, or smelling what is in the area. Any activation of your senses that requires you to locate something in your current environment can help cultivate presence.

When we can harness the power of the present moment, the emotional drudgery of living on autopilot can subside as we realize we can accept what may have traumatized us in the past and live with gratitude, grace, and joy as our true potential emerges. When the stories of the past are no longer attached to the behavior of the present, the stronghold of the personality begins to soften and one's true nature is able to come to the surface.

Being present is an act of trusting in the process of life while releasing the tight grip the memories of our past have on us. This is not to say we should throw all caution to the wind and disconnect from what is occurring, just the opposite. To be present is to be keenly aware of and in connection with yourself so you can sense the subtle energies of change. I can sense this subtle energy internally, as though I'm being forewarned, but it can only occur when I'm present to the moment. Otherwise, I'm not in alignment with the source, or the energy that is greater than me and always trying to steer me in the right direction… if I'm listening.

Presence requires us to become the *inner witness*. In order to be present, we must observe ourselves from a non-judgmental, non-attached, and rational point of view. It is then, within the silent stillness, that we begin to wake up to the present moment, to understand ourselves from the perspective of the witness. With trust, vulnerability, courage, compassion, and a safe outlet to express ourselves, we can begin to realize we are much more than our personality or conditioned behaviors. When we can enter the present moment, in time, we can begin to see that we have a choice in our behavior, instead of always reacting to a situation on autopilot.

As Soul Work deepens, our conscious awareness to make choices becomes easier to have as a default. However, because we are habitual beings with a lifetime of conditional behavior in our system, we will still regularly fall victim to our own habits and patterns, even when we think we've mastered them. It is just a fact of life that because we are spiritual beings having a human experience, we are subject to the default systems of both entities – our conditioned behavior as a human, and our true nature, or essence, as a spiritual being. It's when we learn to integrate these two entities as one that we become liberated. Once this occurs, there's no going back to sleep on autopilot, and yet the work of staying awake never ceases if you are to stay present to the moment.

When present to the moment, we are liberated to express our true nature. We are free to show the world that we're uninhibited by the fear, shame, or guilt of how we think we should express ourselves. Instead, we are empowered to stand tall in our "isness" and express the truth of who we are – unapologetically.

Soul work teaches us that true presence is fleeting, but whenever we feel into our body and sit with the sensations arising, without judgments or stories attached to them, we can begin to soften. We can feel our hearts open and become receptive to the moment, and our minds (as the judge of our perception) can operate from a place of clarity and understanding. Present-time awareness is where peace and harmony exist, and as Byron Katie said in a post on her Facebook page, "Reality is always kinder than the story we tell about it."

CHAPTER 14

ELEMENTS OF SOUL WORK: PRACTICE

Most anything in life that is meaningful, important, or advantageous to a person takes practice. Soul Work is no different. When a person is interested in discovering the truth of who they are, incorporating Soul Work as a way of life is necessary to continue living within that truth. These concepts are one thing to explain and another to live. It comes down to seeing life, and Soul Work, as a practice – a practice of showing up for yourself each day in a way that relies more on being one with life, rather than a conditioned product of it. The practice enables us to be aware of the ego, and the ways in which we latch onto the familiar to give us a sense of safety, love, and acceptance.

With practice, we gain a certain level of skill. This is how we begin to learn living in a human body. While our physical functions appear to be innate, only our initial reflexes are. We have to practice walking, feeding ourselves, drinking from a cup, and talking in order to develop these skills. If fundamental skills are not practiced, we don't function to the best of our abilities. The more practice we partake in, the more our skillset builds. The more skills we acquire, the more confidence we gain. We can apply this same credo to our healing journey. If you've chosen to become consciously more aware of the things that cause you to feel emotionally off-balance, then accountability to show up for yourself and continual practice is required for success in that endeavor.

Practicing Soul Work comes in many layers, and it never ceases. Perhaps you begin your healing journey realizing you feel off-kilter. Simply noticing something is off in you is how it starts. You may live with this feeling for a while, perhaps the majority of your life, until you come across a person or technique that provides you with a different perspective. You may be tired with negative feelings repetitively weighing you down, or you may notice this unease is just how you operate and it's time to make a change. As the saying goes, "What we put our attention on, grows." We can either water our misery like a weed, or we can expand into a richer, more expansive, and more authentic version of ourselves.

On the contrary, we can also go through life in denial that anything is weighing on our psyche. We can do this through coping, which has its foundation in childhood. We can become very good at relying on our unconscious mind to give us the illusion of safety while we act on autopilot. That feeling of spaciness, a mental fog or lethargy can be due to the weight that functioning on autopilot bears. These symptoms may be a clue to do some deep breathing, or laughing or singing, anything to activate the vagus nerve and increase resilience in order to land back in the present moment. Our autopilot defaults have had so much power over us, especially considering that 95% of our brain activity is a subconscious phenomenon, that essentially, we've had ample practice over our lifetimes to remain unconscious to our own conditioned behavior and asleep to a deeper part of ourselves.

In Soul Work, we slowly begin to carefully peel away the many layers that have made us who we are, but we don't lose who we are as a person. We become more of who we are as a true expression of our essence. Our "personhood" can radiate this by more easily accessing joy and happiness, and in time, a greater sense of grace for ourselves and others. In the early years of our lives, we practiced who we came to think we are because of the many conditions set before us as we developed from children into adults.

When we're ready, we can unlearn these conditioned aspects of ourselves and begin to practice new ways of being that are more aligned with the truth of who we are. This is possible, and harder than merely speaking about it. I can attest to it, because I've made a practice of living it, albeit not perfectly, because I am human after all and I'll always be a work in progress.

The easiest and most profound way to realize this is through the sensations that take place in our bodies. When you recognize how your body responds to certain triggers, you can take the opportunity to practice self-compassion by being vulnerable with what is arising, and you can make a choice instead of resorting to the familiarity of your past conditions. You can respond with what feels true, and you can align with your authentic self rather than react to what you are unconsciously fearing due to anger, shame, or guilt. That fear is the young part of ourselves trying to bargain for what he or she never received at an age when it was needed, but we have the power to change the course of our thoughts, and the direction our life may be heading, when we practice conscious awareness.

It's easy to practice what instinctually arises for us. For some, it's the ability to practice different levels of self-preservation, such as ensuring their security with money, eating what's best for their particular body, making a comfortable home, or exercising for health. For others, it may be easier to instinctually practice being of service to others' needs, or being of service to their own, because their survival relies on working together for the common good. Some may find it easier to practice being drawn into the big energy of the room or creating successful collaborations with others. While some things may come easy, it is important for each of us to practice what may not feel easy or instinctual. The reason for this is because as part of the human condition, we are either running away from what we perceive as lacking in ourselves, or we project that void onto others.

Soul Work teaches us to practice compassion in the face of our own healing, which can never truly end. For example, I recently went on a *Mind, Body, Business* retreat in Baja, Mexico, where I received a Reiki treatment. I sensed within me a persistent block to achieving more in my profession than I actually desired, but I just couldn't put my finger on why. Knowing my body would help inform me, I allowed whatever was going to work through me to arise.

What proceeded was a conversation with the Reiki practitioner that led me to understand an implicit belief I have that I cannot be successful without betraying my mother. Well, I didn't see that coming! It made itself known to me through a series of questions that led me directly to this new layer of understanding myself and what I'd been conditioned to believe. The Reiki session allowed the stuck energy in my solar plexus, the area of personal identity, to come up and get released.

I am clearly always practicing and discovering what I don't know about myself, as I occasionally feel the disconnect buzzing around in my body. This is why practicing Soul Work is so important. We must hold ourselves accountable as the layers of healing continue to unfold into truth and potential. Soul Work is a way of life – one that has changed mine for the better, and that I wish to help others discover for themselves.

CHAPTER 15

ELEMENTS OF SOUL WORK: SACRED SPACE

Sacred Space is the cause and effect of Soul Work. It's where all the elements of Soul Work can materialize, as well as what transpires within us from the work being done. It is vital to have a safe space you can call your own, be it physical or mental, because you need to feel safe in order to begin to feel seen.

Our emotional injuries most likely became our wounds because we were not acknowledged by another at one point in early childhood. A lack of safety is initially created when the expressions of our child selves are not seen or heard, thus the psyche imprints the belief that it is unsafe to speak or show up in a situation authentically. There are a litany of ways the psyche copes in order to create a safe place for our bodies to exist, otherwise, how could we, as humans, continue to function in any fashion that felt tolerable?

Before Soul Work, my safe space, unconsciously, was in the appeasement of others. My psyche took on the role of believing if everyone was taken care of, then my mind and nervous system could be at ease. I realized this after fifty years of living this way! Transforming my unconscious safe space of caring for others into the sacred space of caring for myself started with being seen for who I truly was. It began with being witnessed in a way I'd never before been shown or had ever accepted. How I expressed myself was mirrored, and my language was spoken back to me.

Sacred space is what I call home. We must come home to ourselves, and want more for ourselves, in order to follow our true path and discover our purpose in this lifetime – one that is not rife with negativity and pain. For me, it was found in listening, and following a path that creates a connected and engaged sense of wellbeing that is trusted and cared for on the inside. The goal is to feel at home within myself, even when the outside world doesn't share that value.

Moving slowly helps me create that sacred space. I do like a shot of adrenaline, especially when it comes to feeling the energy of lots of people around me, or doing something with speed or precision, like playing Frisbee. But going too fast has often felt like a lack of control for me, as though I'm getting too far away from myself and contacting the present moment becomes more difficult, albeit more pressing.

When my environment, or those in it are moving too fast, it can feel like the ground is shaking and I am out of my body. I may disconnect, remain emotionally distant from both myself and others, and my fears can take over. It is in these types of circumstances – when one feels out of control – that the cultivation of a sacred space becomes necessary in empowering oneself to face and conquer fear. For example, I once had an extreme fear of zip-lining due to the speed, height, and lack of control the sport entails. However, I recently found myself strapped into a harness high up in a forest's canopy as a gift for my husband's birthday.

On the first four lines, I reacted with my familiar, traumatized behavior. I couldn't speak and kept my head down. I listened for clues of safety as I hugged the trunks of trees and I became detached from the outside world, as well as from myself. Doug described my behavior as that of a terrified little girl. However, on the fifth line, I was fed up with the fear, so I made a conscious choice to be present and take it all in. It was the fastest, longest, and highest of all the lines, and yet, I breathed in my surroundings and tapped into my body as I zipped through the trees. My panic dissipated, and I felt calm and at ease, like I was in the eye of the storm.

I felt liberated! I no longer perceived that I was out of control, as I decided to take control of the present moment and join it. I discovered that my sacred space is contacting the quiet stillness inside of myself in order to counteract the speed at which the world may be going by around me. Something I once feared, such as high speeds, doesn't faze me the same way it used to, because I now know how to utilize sacred space within me. The key is connecting with oneself. This becomes my prominent practice during in-flight turbulence!

In Soul Work, it's imperative to find sacred space in order to move courageously through the vulnerability that going inwards entails. Perhaps your sacred space begins with an altar, a special, quiet, and safe space for you, and only you. Or perhaps, your sacred space begins with closing your eyes, taking a deep breath, and identifying a physical sensation. Sacred Space is about building a place of self-respect. A sacred space incorporates the things that were lost at an age when we were too innocent to understand. The worse the trauma, the harder I would imagine the safe place is to find, but possible all the same, as long as you are willing to face your shadow and accept a helping hand.

Most of us spend our lifetimes trying to recreate or find what went missing, but without a sacred space to feel connected to others and aware of ourselves in, our attempts are most often futile. Even those who work their butts off to the point of success, or from fear of failure, can find themselves so far disassociated from the worth of their own heart that to matter feels like an empty hole.

Do you realize how sacred you are? Soul Work guides us back to your sacred selves, back to safety, and back to wholeness. You are a spiritual being having a human experience, and that in itself is a sacred existence. Everything in this world, animate and inanimate, is sacred and deserves the respect of its existence.

CHAPTER 16

TOOLS AND RESOURCES

Just as a hammer and nails are used to build a house, a set of tools is used to fortify an individual's understanding of their soul. The tools I use in Soul Work range from the ancient wisdom of seers and sages, such as with the Enneagram, numerology, and astrology, to the modern insights of psychologists, such as Carl Jung's work with the shadow self and Stephen Porges' Polyvagal Theory.

As well as utilizing the knowledge of those who have historically advanced our collective understanding of the self, I also incorporate tools of my own, such as empathy, deep listening, the four "clairs" (clairaudient, clairsentient, clairvoyant, and claircognizant), guided meditation, channeling, divination tools, energy work, journaling and inquiry prompts, and stream of consciousness writing and speaking.

Beyond these tools is an extensive and individualized list of various resources available to us in our communities as well, such as EMDR, hypnotherapy, traditional therapy and support groups, Shamanic journey, sensory deprivation, yoga, Tai Chi, Reiki, and group circles, to name just a few.

One particular tool that has had a most significant impact on my journey, and one I refer to often with all of my clients, is the

Enneagram. The "Traditional Enneagram" is a psycho-spiritual system and typing tool created by Oscar Ichazo, based on several ancient traditions in combination with his interpretations of personality according to the Enneagram symbol. It is a system that shows us how we filter our lived experiences through the lens of our personality, enabling us to have more insight into ourselves and others. It is my belief that the personality, or conditioned self, does not speak to the soul, and therefore, understanding our personalities as separate better equips us to become aware of our true nature as a whole.

According to Don Richard Riso and Russ Hudson, authors of *The Wisdom of the Enneagram*, the nine different "types," or structures, of the Enneagram correspond to the following *lost messages* from childhood:

1. "You are good."
2. "You are wanted."
3. "You are loved for yourself."
4. "You are seen for who you are."
5. "Your needs are not a problem."
6. "You are safe."
7. "You will be taken care of."
8. "You will not be betrayed."
9. "Your presence matters."

As you read through these *lost messages*, witness their impact on you. Ask yourself, honestly, what childhood message did you miss out on, and how has it affected your beliefs and behavior? Remember, be gentle with yourself and believe in the potential and possibility of Remembering the Truth of Who You Are – your true nature.

The Enneagram, as a tool, is only as good as we are honest in our self-inquiry and self-observations. It offers, with incredible detail and precision, an understanding of why people present as they do in life. More importantly, it offers us a way to recognize and work through the patterns that keep us bound to our conditioned behavior. The Enneagram, if used in such a way, can help guide us towards liberation from our personality.

It is not so much a tool to understand our personality, but a tool to make us aware of our tendencies that get created from the trance of living within the structure of our personality. An example being one of lost childhood messages we missed out on for whatever reason. We either couldn't hear it, or it was never given to us. This lack of messaging is often related to our core wound and our *Basic Fear*. As adults, we project this fear onto others with the unconscious hope that we will finally get what we never received as a child. In time, through Soul Work, we come to realize that no one but ourselves can give us the message we missed out on as a child. By incorporating the elements of Soul Work into life, we can begin to access a deeper part of ourselves so healing may occur.

The Enneagram, along with other wise teachings, such as numerology, shows us that two people of the same birth path, numerologically speaking, will have similar tendencies to what they value in life, it will just express differently according to an individual's perception of their life based on personal experiences growing up. We're all human, so we are composed of all the different aspects of these teachings, however, we tend to be dominant in one aspect. For example, someone on a birth path (numerology) of a "one" will value autonomy at all costs. It might take these individuals years to realize this, especially if their life experiences have conditioned them to be at the beck and call of others. Unless this is explicitly understood by someone on this path, there will likely be frequent upset in their life if they try to create boundaries for themselves after having taught others to depend on them.

These different teachings offer us an understanding of how an individual's personality can be formed, while simultaneously being expressed as a spiritual being housed in a body. There are concrete aspects of these tools that speak to the nature, structure, dimensions, and purpose of their metaphysical science, and there are also the less tangible attributes that are equally as valuable.

The Importance of Knowing Thyself

The reason I am able to write this book is because I've done enough of my own in-depth work that I'm no longer afraid of that which I don't know about myself. I am no longer interested in hiding behind the success of my husband, only to feel inferior within myself. I am at the point where I can embrace my feeling of inferiority, not to him, but rather as the excuse I make to myself, based on the long-held beliefs that many of us carry of not being worthy enough.

It has taken me a decade to get to this point in my life, where I'm now primed to receive ALL OF ME.

This work takes time and patience.

It takes vulnerability and compassion.

It takes reflection and remembrance.

It takes acceptance and allowance.

It takes presence and space.

It takes practice and hard work.

And, I think most importantly, it takes the desire to follow your heart towards your soul along the never-ending journey of Soul Work.

CHAPTER 17

RECONNECT AND REJOICE:
WITH CHOICE AND POTENTIAL

"The aim of life is to live, and to live means to be
Aware, joyously, drunkenly, serenely, divinely Aware."

Henry Miller, *The Wisdom of the Heart*

All humans want to be seen, heard, and to feel safe. When
we're blind to our own needs, we're disconnected from having
a choice in the matter. Not much life force can be activated
from your true being when you're detached from and unaware
of yourself. Before there is any awareness, we are most often
operating on autopilot. While this feels normal and familiar,
it causes us to be in our own way, making it harder to access
real joy or clarity, because the undesirable aspects of ourselves
remain hidden in shadow while the smallest version of ourselves
remains in charge. The soul's energy is re-distributed in ways that
limit our potential, be that outwards through people-pleasing,
projection, or resentment, or inwards with self-loathing, guilt,
or shame. Feelings or states of anxiety, overwhelm, busyness,
avoidance, freneticism, grasping, or numbing are just some of

the ways the underlying feeling of wanting to be seen or heard shows up. Have you noticed this within yourself?

Instead of knowing or being curious about your own needs, do you start doing for others, whether or not you've been asked? If you were honest with yourself, could you see that you might incessantly "do" for others in hopes they'll like/love you? Or do you strive to achieve success with the belief this will make you a good person in the eyes of another? Do you believe you don't have any needs and feel unworthy of care or success? Or maybe, when you look at someone close to you – a partner, child, parent, a friend – you see them for who you want or need them to be for you instead of who they are for them, with all their desires, passions, and individual quirks.

If you don't rock the boat but stay quiet and invisible, do you feel you won't get in trouble with those you care about? Does it make you uncomfortable to express your emotions? Do you find yourself uncomfortable or checked out when someone else is feeling vulnerable and expressing themselves from their heart? These are some examples of the conditional, unconscious programming we may "download" to help us feel safe and loved. Your true authentic form of expression has likely been suppressed by your subconscious, and by all the limitations that are held in your implicit beliefs. A false sense of joy might try to be found through external situations, but joy that originates from within is a joy that is felt in your bones, and in your soul. At its core, this joy is love, gratitude, and potential.

French philosopher, Pierre Teilhard de Chardin, said, "We are spiritual beings having a human experience." This is the premise of my work, not because I adhere to a philosophy, but because I've experienced this concept through its embodiment. I've felt the sensation and connection of experiencing my true nature. It's a feeling of total inner peace, regardless of what may be occurring around me. It is analogous to being in meditation, but in an awakened, alert state of grounded awareness. It is the feeling of understanding – with a piercing clarity – the difference between autopilot and choice, or conditioned behavior and authentic presence. It is making choices that are not influenced by the beliefs that have been ingrained into our nervous systems from past experiences. It is the discovery of our truth in its natural form that leads to liberation. It is the feeling of oneness.

Because we are spiritual beings having a human experience, the human condition will inevitably show up again and again in the form of our personality. As the definition reminds us, personality is the sum total of the physical, mental, emotional, and social characteristics of an individual, amounting to something familiar that we can latch onto – our ego. It is that which encompasses the human condition, including all the facets that make us who we *appear* to be, while bypassing the substance of who we actually are – a soul.

The soul is energy being animated, or the life force contained in our bodies, much like a vehicle houses a motor, or a lake, river, or ocean houses water. A container holds the form, and the form is activated through life force, through the animation of molecules, and through the conduction of energy. The form however, because it is mercurial, shows up in many ways. The soul's form can shift in its expression, or as Kahlil Gibran says, "Your body is the harp of your soul, and it is yours to bring forth sweet music from it or confused sounds."

As I see it, the soul is our true nature, and as human beings, we each have the potential to recognize this sensation and experience it if we do the hard work of honest self-exploration. It's a never-ending journey to work on remembering and reclaiming our true nature, and it requires practice to maintain the spiritual thread that keeps us connected to the true reflection of ourselves, as well as something greater than ourselves. This is God, Gaia, our creator, our father, our mother, our Great Spirit, our Ground of Being, or Yahweh – it is whatever your name is for that which is not tangible, and yet holds the key to all that is.

Our souls are born into our bodies – or our containers – so we can learn how to navigate our spiritual beings that reside within each of us in their truest forms. We learn how we are "supposed" to act through the development of a personality, or an ego in relation to our own worlds. However, we are not our personalities. *This is just who I am* is a limiting statement. This implicit belief is how our conditioned behavior begins to take shape.

Humans are conditioned to learn how to react through their relationships with others. In the earliest years of our lives, our brains do not offer us the capacity to respond through conscious thought. Young children can only react to situations that teach them how to get what they need, which, ultimately, is love and safety. These two basic needs are satisfied through a secure attachment with a primary caregiver. While everyone's experiences are unique unto themselves, the psyche looks for ways to adapt to situations in order to feel loved and safe. The human body has the intelligence, or the all-knowing truth of an individual's soul, to equip us with the ability to survive even the most horrendous of situations.

The nervous system, specifically the vagus nerve, plays a significant part in how a child reacts to a situation in which they are deprived of love and safety, or a secure attachment. The vagus nerve, the largest nerve in the body, is connected to all of our major organs and is responsible for regulating the nervous system and its response to trauma. Establishing an insecure attachment with a primary caregiver, for example, whether as a result of trauma, emotional injury, neglect, or abuse, directly impacts an individual's ability to regulate their nervous system, causing them to be stuck in a fight, flight, freeze, or fawn response.

As we mature, and hopefully regain access to the curiosities and imaginations of our child selves, we can learn to understand and consciously experience our conditioned behaviors and modes of reactivity in a newly enlightened state. With the elements of Soul Work in our tool belt, we can actively heal the wounds, making it possible to reverse the damage done to our nervous systems and regain control of our emotional responses to stress. As we are always in our own way of seeing beyond our defensive (and familiar) limitations, guidance from another, combined with time and practice, can help each of us immensely in accessing our true nature. When we become aware of our true nature, we can act from choice, instead of reacting from conditioned behavior.

This is our challenge as humans living the human condition. *Condition* being the operative word. The meaning behind the word *condition* originates from an agreement. In some cases, it is necessary to agree upon and understand the guidelines for defining and labeling something, such as with a medical condition. However, conditions can become detrimental when the behaviors that have been ingrained in us as children through the process of conditioning cause us internal or external conflict. This can be very subtle and difficult to become aware of because these conditions lie deep within our nervous systems and manifest in how all of us function on a societal level.

The human brain's use of its subconscious abilities – which, as stated previously is estimated to be 95% of the time – is actually a wonderful and intelligent survival mechanism. Scientists have agreed that until seven years old, our minds are in a theta brainwave state – remaining connected to one's internal world. It can be described as a realm of imagination and daydreaming, and while in this state, a child is unable to show signs of critical thinking or rational thought. The influence of this state of mind can extend up to the age of twelve, when the *logic stage* of brain development begins and critical thinking arises.

Therefore, it is safe to say that what a child experiences at this time in their life is analogous to the creation of their internal hardware, which lays the foundation for how a child communicates, socializes, and relates to others. This phase of development varies for every individual based on the dynamics of their home environment and how they are cared for by their providers. Even children in the same family will develop their hardware differently based on direct personal experience of their own unique upbringing.

The point to realize here is that this is the time the subconscious is being formed. Another way to put this is that the experiences of a child between the ages of zero and seven inform the subconscious. And since we live 95% of the time in our subconscious, the norms we learned in this very susceptible time of brain growth become our autopilot function as adults. This is what we default to on a regular basis in how we perceive life, ourselves, and others. This is the formation of our personality and how we come to know who we think we are.

It's as though we get our download in early childhood and then we go out into the world programmed to perform according to our specific hardware. Just as a computer houses different programs, humans have specific programs as well, such as coping with stress or the pursuit of passions. These *programs* express themselves differently. This is our individuality. Most of us go through our entire lives behaving from the conditions laid down in the first decade of life, with little awareness that this is how we function.

The day we consciously choose to question our own motives, our own behaviors, and our own thoughts, is the day we begin to wake up to the truth of who we are, individually and collectively. It is through allowing inward reflection to take place that we can rationally discern our realities from the familiar stories of our past. Ironically, this place of inwardness – whether evoked through silent and still meditation, conscious breath work, or a focused task, to name only a few methods – is the same theta state that those familiar stories were written in as children.

The difference between the theta state of a young child and the theta state accessed by an adult, however, is the use of critical thinking. Using logic is not an option for a young child in rationalizing the experiences that are shaping them. When we access our theta states as adults, with the intention of acceptance and allowance behind the practice, we can begin to wake up to the present moment and witness who we truly are.

Once we begin to see that we are an accumulation of experiences, we get to rewrite the past with present-time awareness. This takes time though. Our bodies have been formatted on a cellular level to take in past information and store it like an operating unit. If we never make contact with our hard drive, so to speak, it will keep us running on automatic while our subconscious makes choices for us.

We come to believe this is who we are because we show up in the same body, doing the same things, day in and day out. Our actions may look different from one day to the next, depending on how we animate in a particular situation, environment, or relationship, but the behavior still derives from the deep programming of past survival mechanisms. This developmental function may be necessary for a young person to establish a sense of safety in the familiar, but when we continue to act and behave from the perception of our child-self, our adult-self gets distorted. This can become the cause behind coping behaviors, such as drug and alcohol use, unhealthy distractions, and workaholism, as well as negative or painful emotional states, such as anxiety, rage, and depression.

The list of problems that can arise due to adverse childhood experiences, and the insecure egos and unhealthy nervous systems that develop as a result, is extensive. While the characters in our lives may change, the behavior rarely does, *unless* we turns towards ourselves with an intimate perspective. When we begin to get curious about how and why we act the way we do, then lean into the areas of life that lack harmony, the reward is liberation from the familiar chains of childhood. As a result, the adult self can inhabit the adult body in a state of conscious awareness.

Soul Work defies habits and familiarity – it just *IS*. Another subtle quality of recognizing oneself as a spiritual being having a human experience is the ability to just *BE* with what is and not infuse story into a situation. I've learned that in order to become consciously aware of, and make contact with, one's true self, and to surrender to divine order, a safe space is required to witness what is being felt and/or discovered. Any stories we use to define ourselves are just that – stories. The stronghold of the personality tells us these stories are true. It takes trust to know that what you feel deep inside your heart, beyond the familiarity of your stories, is a true reflection of your soul.

I call it a story because the memories that make up our human condition stem from the singular point of view of the individual experiencing them, while the implicit beliefs that manifest from our individual stories act like a personal mythology. Until we begin to pull apart these outdated stories, we will continue to try and manipulate reality to fit into what we deem as safe and comfortable.

The most impactful story from my childhood was a particular moment in which I felt vulnerable and didn't get what I needed to feel safe. My four-year-old self needed to be seen and heard by my mother, but I was ignored, so my psyche created a story based on an implicit belief that expressing myself does not garner my safety, but taking care of others does. I was conditioned by this experience not to use my voice, at least not in a way that would advocate for my own needs.

Nothing spoken by my mother explicitly told me speaking wasn't safe. My mind unconsciously created a story that gave me the illusion I would be safe and feel loved if I didn't speak up for myself, because when I tried to, the most significant person in my life didn't respond to me. Now, that doesn't mean my mother was intentionally trying to disregard me, but my undeveloped mind was more concerned with surviving and incapable of rational thought. My developing mind created a story that defined my behavior as the problem, rather than risk seeing my mother as the responsible one.

This is the human condition in a nutshell. When trauma, big or small, occurs in a child's life, they are not equipped to know how to respond. In order to survive, they rewrite the moment their nervous systems were shocked and make it about their own behavior. In my case, I was not seen or heard in a moment of need, which played into the limiting belief that I was not worthy of having needs of my own, despite the innocence of the act that precipitated this belief. I say it was innocent because my mother was not acting out of malice. It was a situation in which I needed boundaries and to be consoled in my upset, but neither happened. Perhaps my mom was too tired, or distracted, or she just wanted the task of dressing her child to be over with. Maybe she thought I was simply having a tantrum and would just get over it if she calmly didn't respond.

From the point of view of a child who needs to be attached to a caregiver in order to survive, appeasing my mother's needs in that moment took precedence over my own, and so my implicit belief was written. In childhood, creating familiar stories from moments of emotional injury is an effective survival technique with the purpose of maintaining a connection with one's caregiver, albeit now a conditional one.

In discussions I've had with my mom as I was coming to terms with the stories of my past, it was revealed to me that this was my mother's generational trauma being passed down to me. She too was not seen nor heard in moments of need as a child. This is the case for most of us, the experience just looks different. I've realized, and accepted, that the reason she didn't console me was because she couldn't contact that place inside of her that also needed consoling.

What cannot be contacted within ourselves, cannot be given to another – because there is no point of origin to pull from. And because I am human, just as my mother is, the stories that were *programmed* into my subconscious can come out of nowhere, at any time, to pull me back into believing it's not safe to speak my truth. The difference between who I am now, and who I was before, is awareness. I'm now quick to notice this old, familiar pattern, and I have an opportunity to decide if I'll succumb to habit or take a stand and authentically express myself.

While I have a much better handle on my triggers that are based in childhood perceptions, I now find myself more amused than distraught when I see them rear their frightened mask. It takes a keen level of discernment – acquired with time and the practice of Soul Work – to sift through what can be learned from a situation versus what jolts my nervous system into believing I'm not being seen or cared for by another.

Truth is, as long as I can remember to come home to myself by connecting to my true nature, that quiet, uncluttered place inside me, I have the ability to bring myself into a state of homeostasis, allowing me to experience an engaging and safe connection with myself and others. I find this through meditation, hot tubs, and meaningful conversations with others. Dancing, laughing, live music, and having pure fun for the sake of experiencing joy with others makes me feel alive. I like to surround myself with nature's beauty and the clever curiosity of animals, because they help me experience a childlike innocence.

I've learned that taking care of my own needs has to be a priority, or else my authentic compassion and the desire I have to take care of others becomes tarnished by my implicit beliefs and conditioned behaviors. It is easy, however, to become complacent and succumb to the numbing feeling of being less alive in my mind, body, and spirit. This is why community is so important, something I have to actively create or become a part of to hold myself accountable in my own continuous practice of Soul Work.

An important step in seeing and accepting ourselves is having our true nature witnessed and accepted by others.

The idea of being able to fully express yourself sounds desirable, but the path to getting there and actually allowing it to happen is an entirely different ball game. It requires looking at the conditioned behaviors that have carried you this far in life and noticing how they get in your way. Awareness of ourselves, especially in relation to others, is the key to lifting the veil of our conditioned behaviors, re-activating our life force, and living to our highest potential. Until we can come to a place within ourselves to recognize our own conditioned behavior, we will continue to behave in ways that feel familiar – not healthy, but familiar – and try to 'adjust' someone else's expressions to meet our needs.

Rather than hearing another's needs, wants, and desires from a place of compassion, it becomes more about what we need from their interaction to feel seen, heard, or safe. Without this awareness, communication becomes ineffective, which often leads to frustrations, acknowledged or not. Except in circumstances involving extreme forms of abuse, the relationships we have with those closest to us are most often the perfect place to begin our own healing, as long as we have the courage to scrutinize ourselves first before we begin assigning blame or projecting our conditioning onto another. This takes work, patience, vulnerability, and most of all, it takes compassion for yourself and for others.

Many areas in life outside of ourselves can give us the feeling of wholeness or competence, which is great and necessary. However, we are all originally wounded in our relationships as children, most often by our primary caregivers. This could be a wounding from a *small t* trauma, such as being ignored during a time of emotional need, or a *big T* trauma, such as with physical or sexual abuse. Emotional wounding, either way, happens in relation to another. This is why our best chance at healing that wound as adults is most often in our relationships, and not necessarily with those who directly caused our wounds (especially for those who have experienced abuse, where it may be best to avoid contact with their abuser).

I've come to realize that in order for me to feel safe, I projected my need for connection, engagement, trust, and care onto others so I could experience what was empty, or uncared for, inside of me. Although I am a genuinely compassionate and caring human being, and do like to be in service to others, these qualities can become distorted and problematic when the appeasement of others' needs come at the expense of my own. This inhibits my ability to establish real connection, authentic engagement, trustworthy confidence, and mutual care.

I see these conditions unfold primarily in relationships that have the most meaning to me (intimate, familial, professional, or interpersonal). For example, what prompted my choice to be my daughter's full-time caregiver after the accident that paralyzed her was the amount of compassion I feel for her and the unfortunate limitations that injury puts on any person. My compassion, however, can also get clouded by my implicit belief that taking care of others, and not myself, ensures my own safety. This is a very difficult situation as it pertains to my own child, but also represents a codependency, enmeshment, and a comfort in the familiar for me. This has been a curse and a fortune for both my daughter and myself.

I've made myself available to her in order to make her life more comfortable, and to help her navigate through the tough times successfully. I remained available for her and continued to tend to her needs to make her transitions through high school, college, and careers easier. As a mother, I sought to take an active role in making what was familiar to her safe. I saw her and heard her as well as I could, as she too needed to find her own voice. After taking care of her for four years in a purely conditioned state of mind, then discovering my true self through Soul Work so I may finally attend to own needs, I've become aware of the delicate balance between meeting the needs of my daughter because I've chosen to, and meeting my own needs because I desire spiritual liberation.

The very fact that we inhabit our bodies on earth at this time is a cause for celebration, a cause for respecting and acknowledging our duty as humans to live in the joy that is available to us. Joy is an essential quality of being human. It is our human experiences that leave us with the feeling of being robbed of this spiritual joy, so we use any superficial means possible to try and get back to that lost feeling, but really, it already resides deep within. It just becomes harder to witness because it gets covered up by shame, guilt, prejudice or sorrow, and we come to believe this is the reality of what normal is. In order not to feel these negative states anymore, we all too often resort to numbing them, shutting them down, escaping, isolating, becoming overly involved with things, projects, or people, all the while denying what and where the source of joy comes from – quietly inside of our natural being.

Deep inside each of us, all our soul asks for is pure, unadulterated acknowledgment of its existence. One way to experience the simple joy of existence is in a state of presence where genuine compassion, generosity, oneness, kindness, and love for all resides. We must turn inward and face the shadow that casts a need to hide, or run, or self-medicate, or do too much, whether it be socially, mentally, or physically, and acknowledge what has been amiss all this time. We just might find that what was missing was in ourselves all along.

Complacency in our conditioning can fill the place of needs and create a void inside of us. It has been through my own exploration and discovery of my deeper self that I've come to recognize when complacency is running the show. I now realize I have a choice in the matter. *This is liberation.* This is what I am passionate about teaching and guiding others towards. I want others to experience the same liberation I have.

Because of Soul Work, I am now free to live in my potential, in the possibilities of choice and the expansion of myself.

CHAPTER 18

OFFER: THE FULL CIRCLE

"Circles, like the soul, are never-ending and turn
round and round without a stop."

Ralph Waldo Emerson,
"Circles" in *Essays: First Series*

"You've changed," my mother said.

"How?" I asked. "Why do you say that?"
"You've become the person you're meant to be."

I believe in divine order. I believe things happen as they're supposed to, when they're supposed to. There are four Native American Indian Spirituality Laws that express "Nothing happens for no reason" because "No one rain drop, anywhere in the world, accidentally falls in the wrong place." When you embrace this philosophy, it's easier to handle and confidently look at what's happening to you, be thankful for what has already happened, and happy for what's going to happen next.

The four laws state:

First: "The person you meet is the right one."

Second: "What happens is the only thing that can happen."

Third: "Every moment when something starts is the right time."

Fourth: "What is over is over."

This doesn't mean what happens doesn't hurt, but in time, when a sense of understanding can be drawn from any experience, the darkness lightens and clarity transpires. (https:// halaihealingplace.com/blog/affirmatiions/native-american -indian-spirituality/)

What would it be like if we lived from a place of complete, undisturbed existence without the feelings of judgment from ourselves or others clouding our path? Can you imagine what it would look and feel like to unapologetically show up in life in full expression of *you*? To have the anxiety of what others are thinking or saying about how you show up drop away? How about not having to work yourself into the ground, and realizing what it means to relax, knowing when enough is enough? Or how about standing up for what you believe in and verbalizing it without the fear of being told you're wrong? How would it feel to fully express yourself in your relationships, your career, or in your contributions to life? It might feel pretty awesome, huh?!

It would look something like peace. This may be an ideal view, but it is attainable, and not just with wishful thinking or positive affirmations, but through the hard work of seeing our dark shadows and coming into the light of who we are. We are beings who deserve to be happy, but more importantly, to feel the pure essence of our being.

Our experiences shape our lives, and we become ingrained and caught up in the stories that gave us a sense of self as a child. To never question or witness our own behavior as adults, or to act without honest integrity in how we show up in the world, imprisons us to the conditions of our personalities.

To never confront ourselves leaves us living on a treadmill of delusion, in which we continue to chase or run from our illusions of inadequacy, doubt, shame, fear, or fill-in-the-blank. The need to cope through denial and or addiction only digs a deeper hole for us. We can either dig ourselves out with awareness, acknowledgment, truth, honesty, vulnerability, and compassion, or we can dig down further through addiction, judgment, denial, shame, and blame. Life isn't as hard as we make it out to be, but to live in the delusion that all is good, while at the same time coping through it, only leads to the blind leading the blind.

While my life has been a wild ride of non-stop crises of one tragedy after another, crisis lets you know what you're made of, and I've been able to transform my trauma into joy, aliveness, purpose, and potential. I've had the example of my parents to follow for strength and tenacity when it comes to enduring such hardship. They just celebrated their sixty-sixth wedding anniversary, and while my dad has slowed down at the age of ninety-one, my eighty-five-year-old mother is still up for travel and adventure wherever she can find it.

A tree with strong roots produces a strong trunk with beautiful, flowing, healthy branches and leaves. It learns to endure and go with the flow of storms that pass by, through the nourishment and stability found at its base. It graciously sways with each gust of wind that tries to break it. In order to withstand the frequent assaults of nature's challenges, be that wind, rain, fire, or erosion, it must always pull strength from the solid foundation established in its roots. The tree knows how to survive, and is a product of receiving what serves its growth. Human life is no different. The beauty of aliveness spreads its joy like the branches and leaves of a tree, and the strength to grow into the potential inside all of us is in our spiritual foundations.

This is how I see my life. Whether or not I received what I really needed in my youth, which was emotional attunement, I did receive love – love that established a baseline of caring. Through Soul Work, I relearned to trust the solid foundation of where I came from, storms and all, and use engagement as a way of offering compassion when the weather is more severe than desired. This is part of my "intenseness". I take opportunities seriously, in that if I have a reason for participating, I'll put myself in the position of gaining as much as I can from it. Otherwise, I feel I'm just wasting time. If the work or situation I'm involved in is something I know I or someone else will benefit from, my willingness and openness are heightened even more. It's this energy I brought into my own journey, as well as what I bring into working with my clients. I feel strongly that to choose to do something is to make the commitment to carry it out to fruition.

When my mother noticed my transformation and acknowledged that I've become the person I was meant to be, it dawned on me that I've come full-circle from my emotionally wounded four-year-old self. This is generational healing! Through my work, I've had some good conversations with my mom, and she could see the direct correlation of her own wounding being passed down to me. With the admission of her own pain, she came to realize mine. For my mother to say to me, "You've become the person you're meant to be," is valid evidence of healing, on both sides. She and I showed up in life in similar ways – we didn't have many needs, or at least, we believed we didn't. The once unseen, personal wounds of both my mother and myself have now been seen, through her eyes and mine, and as a result, she is now witnessing her daughter engaged in a life that helps bring people to an understanding of themselves.

The person I am meant to be is fully and heartily immersed in the exciting and engaging adventure of life. For me, this is not a wild and extreme involvement in, say X-sports, but the wild and compelling possibilities that live in the expansiveness of becoming *all that we are meant to be* by integrating our hearts with our minds and bodies.

For me, this began with self-compassion, with an understanding of the human condition, and an awareness of how we all individually fit into the psycho-spiritual dimensions of being human. I believe that without learning self-compassion, nothing we do in life will ever feel good enough because we're not extending compassion for the hardships of the human condition to ourselves. Let me help you relearn and embody what it means to be *enough*, by guiding you on an exploration of your true self.

I present to you the opportunity to sit back, with me as your loving guide, and take an intimate perspective into your own life, one I'm certain has been fraught with some degree of confusion, sadness, denial, anxiety, anger, despondency, guilt, bitterness, mania, and doubt. The spectrum of human emotion is expansive and complex, and I want to acknowledge that what I offer is not easy, nor is it realized and then over with.

What I can promise is that through practicing Soul Work, and in witnessing oneself in true form, we can begin to trust in the unknown. We can learn from the nuances and subtleties of what we can hear in the silence – the brief pause between breaths in which you can reflect on how you show up in any particular moment – by conditions or by choice. Until then, it can feel like an enormous weight bearing down on your chest and completely draining you of your life force, with nowhere to go but to cope. It can feel like walking on a contained bed of water, always beneath you, but never offering a solid footing.

If you don't take that first step into the space of inward uncertainty, then life can lay dormant, waiting for the day you finally do, a day when you become fully expressed as the truest you. The revelation of self can take on many forms once the bubble is pierced. Allow me to take you on a trip of a lifetime through the unleashing of an Intimate Perspective with your life. It might just be all you've ever needed. It was for me.

I found healing, growth, and the ability to experience true joy when I finally leaned into the unknown and discovered Soul Work. Because of the way I've always seen life, with the vibrations that exist beneath its surface, and with a curious mind and a penchant for awareness (some would call it common sense or emotional intelligence), I've realized my purpose is to help others by offering them clarity where confusion may lie, a calmness to replace anxiety, and compassion for the grieving, the vulnerable, and the lost. My intuitive ways of resonating with life, whether in its physical or spiritual form, as well as my personal work with the Enneagram, numerology, and several other tools, resources, and schools of thought, enables me to offer you a better sense of yourself. I can help you gain more confidence in facing inward into areas that you may have avoided in the past.

This avoidance may stem merely from a lack of awareness, or more accurately, from your essential self-having not been mirrored, or having been destructively mirrored in the form of denial, gaslighting, or neglect to your needs as a child. In mirroring one another, we get to have a sense of self and learn about who we are through reflection.

When we have the opportunity to catapult ourselves into this type of awakening, we can do things beyond our wildest expectations. And while there are many successful, accomplished, well-meaning people in the world, there is also often a disconnect amongst them from their personal feelings and their ability to contact them or stay with them for an extended period of time. I believe it is crucial for each of us to observe ourselves – our implicit beliefs, our conditioned behaviors, and our relationships with others – with the guidance of a compassionate witness in order to come to an honest depiction of who we know ourselves to be in our heart of hearts.

To show up in a world where your actions are predicated on the response of another makes for a life half lived. Unfortunately, this cycle has become the way we humans operate. However, with curiosity, desire, and the elements of practicing Soul Work, there is a way to break this cycle and live as the fully expressed being you were born to be. To be in awe of life is living in the awareness of all it has to offer, while realizing that much of life will never be fully understood.

Life encompasses everything. When you can embody this truth and trust in the process of life, there is no better medicine to receive. If we could all show up to a situation with the intention of operating on the basis of our true nature, then the world would be filled with self-actualized human beings living out their prescribed purposes to their highest potentials. It's when purpose can be sustained with passion that life becomes truly joyful. We humans have the capacity to do just that. It is the intention to live deliberately and "on purpose" that propels us to the pinnacle of our individual lives.

I know from experience it can't be done alone. Yes, it is each of our own work to feel through the pain, but the guidance and witnessing of at least one other is what helps us dig ourselves out of the trenches of self-deceit. Self-inquiry is not for the weak of heart, but it is an opportunity to recognize the facade we've used to cover our "weak-feeling" hearts through years of building up defenses. Most of the people who come to see me feel stuck in their life and sense there is something more for them, but they're unable to put their finger on it or they don't know how to take action. I help them discover and understand where the missing pieces lie within themselves.

The road to learning how to discern the child-self from the adult-self may be long, and even upon discovering your True Nature it can remain mercurial, but once you realize you have a choice in how you move forward, the empowerment Soul Work brings is enduring. Once discovered, your true self is always available to you when you look inward for it. Your soul's potential is waiting to be activated, and it's your choice to initiate the process and dive into the practice.

My degree is in Child Development, but my wisdom is from a place deep inside. When you come to me confused, stuck, or frustrated with how you or others are showing up in your life, I will listen to you. I will guide you to see yourself and show you how to discern between the stories you believe and the reality of the present. This can be a tricky thing to discern, but I know from experience that with self-compassion, vulnerability, and a safe place to confront yourself, anything is possible.

It is through courage and trust, in and from ourselves, that we gain the confidence to go out in the world and behave in accordance with our true nature – in accordance with our soul agreement. It is with full belief and conviction, deep in my soul, that I believe these words to be true, especially when I look at the many facets of life, and the many ways in which we humans accomplish wonderful, phenomenal feats.

I see how we are multidimensional, spiritual beings, and at the same time, we're humans affected by our conditions. I see how fear, anxiety, anger, and rage can wreak havoc on our ability to show up in our bodies and function in our full capacity as pure extracts of light. I can see how procrastination and self-doubt can run us in circles, while chasing the dream. And I can see that with silence, listening, and the courage to confront ourselves, the ability to remember who we are is available to us all.

Through my own practice of Soul Work, I've come to realize and embody the truth of who I am. The very fact that I've written this book to be read by others is an example of realizing that my words do matter, and I am no longer afraid to share them. I would also not be able to facilitate groups or work successfully with one-on-one clients if I still believed my words didn't matter. Soul Work transformed me, and I believe it can do the same for you.

You are your greatest gift!

Being able to fully express yourself in life is your birthright. To step into your authentic expression can seem daunting. It may seem unattainable, a feat achievable for only a select few, but the transformation can belong to anyone who is curious enough to begin. The process can look different for everyone, but the results are the same: Liberation and Potential! For me, it is what gives my life its richness. I am on a continual journey, and so are you. It takes dedication, and this book is a symbol of my own dedication in reclaiming my truth as I raised myself up in it. The climb never ceases, and it will always be a choice just how high you choose to go in reaching your full potential.

With this knowledge, awareness, and outlook on life, I can help guide you towards uncovering your truth. How far you take it is up to you, but I know it's worth the exploration.

And so it is.

EVERYTHING

by Angela DeSalvo

Everything we ever held in our hands
Has ripped my heart open.
It has debunked the idea
that all is perfect and just as you imagined it should be.

Everything that has ever been held in my hands
Feels as though it has been ripped out
And taken from me in some unfair, fucked-up sense of
"This is just the way it is."

I could see it this way,
Or I could realize
Or maybe pretend, that everything
I've ever held in my hands is an act
And an offering of Love at its highest existence.

I could believe that everything I've ever held in my hands
Has the beauty and possibility of being just that,
Beauty and possibility.
I could feel it all—

That everything I've ever held in my hands
Has crushed me to smithereens and
Has built me to heights never known possible.

I will say that Everything I've ever held in my hands
Has become an extension of the pure and purposeful Love
That is needed and was meant to be—

So, that Everything I Ever Hold
In my hands, will
Flourish.

CONCLUSION

I continue to find my voice in those who speak the same language as me. Not necessarily the English language, but the soulful, spiritual language of self.

If, like me, you desire a deeper understanding of your true essence, I encourage you to seek guidance and trust in the process of life.

If you are interested in connecting with me as your guide, exploring what aspects of yourself feel out of alignment, and embarking on a journey towards who you truly are, please contact me.

I offer each new client a free, 30-minute Clarity Call.

You may reach me through my website. Know that I look forward to hearing from you.

www.angeladesalvo.net

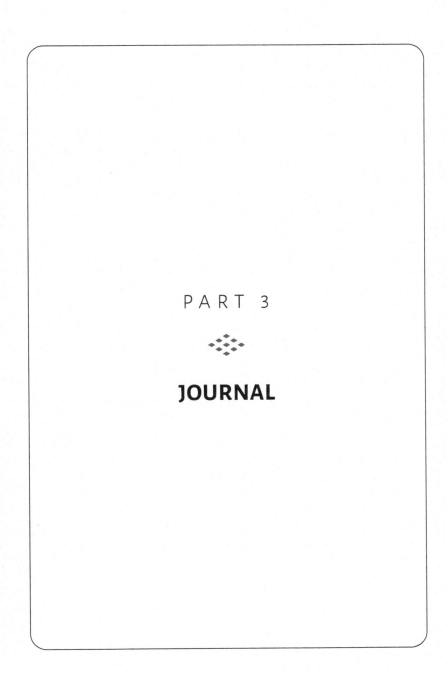

PART 3

JOURNAL

JOURNAL PART 1:
AN INTIMATE PERSPECTIVE

Open-ended Prompts: As you read my story and reflect on your own, use this space to help you navigate and process any emotions or memories that arise for you.

You may choose to free-write, jot down notes, draw/doodle, or leave each space blank as you simply ponder what each word means to you.

Remember

_____

_____

_____

_____

_____

_____

_____

_____

_____

_____

_____

_____

_____

Accept

Face

Witness

Acknowledge

Embrace

_____

_____

_____

_____

_____

_____

_____

_____

_____

_____

_____

_____

_____

_____

_____

_____

_____

_____

_____

_____

_____

_____

_____

_____

_____

Discover

JOURNAL PART 2:
THE WORK

Applying the Elements of Soul Work at Home

Journal Exercises: Set aside 15 minutes of uninterrupted, focused time for each writing prompt.

Do not hesitate as your words unravel onto paper. Let them fall from you, unedited and unrestrained, like a continuous waterfall of your truest self.

Your responses may help you process your truth. They may bring to light new insights as you dive deeper into the intimate process of Transformational Soul Work, or you may wish to bring them along to one of our sessions to help us guide your journey towards liberation together.

Connection

The importance of connecting with others in order to connect with the Self. Begin to witness your behaviors and patterns when around others.

What makes you feel connected to others and to yourself?

Where or with whom do you feel most connected?

What causes you to disconnect from yourself, others, or your surroundings?

_____

_____

_____

_____

_____

_____

_____

_____

_____

_____

_____

_____

_____

_____

_____

_____

_____

_____

_____

_____

_____

_____

Connecting with Trust

Have faith in the unknown and channel confidence in the natural process of life.

What does trust mean to you?

What enables you to trust your environment and others in it?

_____

_____

_____

_____

_____

_____

_____

_____

_____

_____

_____

_____

_____

_____

_____

_____

_____

_____

_____

_____

_____

_____

If trust is established, where would curiosity take you?

Connecting with Vulnerability

The healing journey is a vulnerable one. The word itself relates to wounding or injury.

In what kind of circumstances do you feel most vulnerable?

_____

_____

_____

_____

_____

_____

_____

_____

_____

_____

_____

_____

_____

_____

_____

_____

_____

_____

_____

What feels uneasy about being emotionally exposed?

What happens when you allow yourself to be seen?

_____

_____

_____

_____

_____

_____

_____

_____

_____

_____

_____

_____

_____

_____

_____

_____

_____

_____

_____

_____

_____

_____

_____

_____

Connecting with Courage

Putting pen to paper is an act of courage – allow it to take you to places unknown. Be unattached to the outcome.

What are you most afraid of?

_____

_____

_____

_____

_____

_____

_____

_____

_____

_____

_____

_____

_____

_____

_____

_____

_____

_____

_____

_____

_____

_____

When was a time you felt courageous?

What allowed you to have courage?

Connecting with Compassion

Extending warmth or care to yourself or another's suffering. Be gentle here, most people don't offer themselves compassion. It's okay, try it.

Is there a time in your life when you needed compassion but it was missing, either from someone else or for yourself?

_____

_____

_____

_____

_____

_____

_____

_____

_____

_____

_____

_____

_____

_____

_____

_____

_____

_____

What would have changed if compassion was present?

What would your child-self have needed in that moment?

Self-Care

The importance of making one's own needs a priority.

What do I need?

_____

_____

_____

_____

_____

_____

_____

_____

_____

_____

_____

_____

_____

_____

_____

_____

_____

_____

_____

_____

_____

_____

_____

_____

_____

What does taking care of myself look like?

How did I take care of myself yesterday?

How can I take care of myself today?

Caring for the Mind

It's easy to contact the mind to pull out what we know, or the familiar, but to discern — or to have a proper perspective of reality — requires an awareness of what is present, or what IS now.

How has your "hardware" been "programmed" by your childhood?

_____

_____

_____

_____

_____

_____

_____

_____

_____

_____

_____

_____

_____

_____

_____

_____

_____

_____

_____

What does acting on autopilot look like for you?

What behaviors have you been conditioned to perceive as,
"This is just the way I am."

What does it look like for your adult-self to make conscious choices, right now? Without judgement, ask yourself, What IS NOW?

_____

_____

_____

_____

_____

_____

_____

_____

_____

_____

_____

_____

_____

_____

_____

_____

_____

_____

_____

_____

_____

_____

_____

_____

Caring for the Body

Pick a part of your body that aches or feels constricted. Place your hand on that part of your body, close your eyes, and ask, "What do I need to remember?" When you feel ready, begin writing in response. This could be an important aspect of yourself that you've rejected for a long time.

What kind of physical movements make you feel most at ease?

_____

_____

_____

_____

_____

_____

_____

_____

_____

_____

_____

_____

_____

_____

_____

_____

When you use your body in whatever way feels good to you, whether it be through yoga, walking, dancing, painting, singing, or exercise — what allows the expression of your inner world to be brought outwards?

_____

_____

_____

_____

_____

_____

_____

_____

_____

_____

_____

_____

_____

_____

_____

_____

_____

_____

_____

_____

_____

_____

Caring for the Heart

Survival mode often manifests in defending our hearts, while an open heart liberates our potential.

When emotionally triggered, what are your defense mechanisms?

_____

_____

_____

_____

_____

_____

_____

_____

_____

_____

_____

_____

_____

_____

_____

_____

_____

_____

_____

_____

_____

With a fully courageous and open heart, how do you envision yourself responding instead?

_____

_____

_____

_____

_____

_____

_____

_____

_____

_____

_____

_____

_____

_____

_____

_____

_____

_____

_____

_____

_____

_____

_____

What's easier for you — giving or receving?

Do you have ulterior motives to giving or receiving?

Reflection and Remembrance

Face the past. Embrace the past. Remember the truth of who you are.

When you reflect on your childhood, what do you remember?

_____

_____

_____

_____

_____

_____

_____

_____

_____

_____

_____

_____

_____

_____

_____

_____

_____

_____

_____

_____

What is your first memory?

What is the most profound memory you have from early childhood? From adolescence? As an adult? From yesterday?

Observe your actions, your patterns, your habits in thought and body without judgement. What begins to arise when you intentionally witness yourself? This is the opposite of autopilot.

_____

_____

_____

_____

_____

_____

_____

_____

_____

_____

_____

_____

_____

_____

_____

_____

_____

_____

_____

_____

Acceptance/Allowance

To receive or permit something, either concrete, abstract, or elusive in nature.

As you go through the elements of Soul Work with patience and intention, this step becomes more attainable. When you can accept yourself, you can discern between your conditioned behavior and choosing to allow what needs to arise. This is where transformation begins to occur.

What do you have a hard time accepting about your past, present and future?

What holds you back from the full expression of your true self?

_____
_____
_____
_____
_____
_____
_____
_____
_____
_____
_____
_____
_____
_____
_____
_____
_____
_____
_____
_____
_____
_____
_____

What are you beginning to allow as you consider what trust, vulnerablity, courage, and compassion mean to you? As you consider what it means for you to take care of your mind, body, and heart? As you reflect and remember?

Presence

Notice with intention. Be the Witness.

Take a walk with child-like wonder and let your curiosity lead the way.

_____

_____

_____

_____

_____

_____

_____

_____

_____

_____

_____

_____

_____

_____

_____

_____

_____

_____

Take a deep breath.

Describe in real-time what thoughts and sensations are flowing through you as you write about them.

_____

_____

_____

_____

_____

_____

_____

_____

_____

_____

_____

_____

_____

_____

_____

_____

_____

_____

_____

_____

_____

_____

_____

_____

_____

_____

_____

_____

_____

_____

What does the pen feel like in your hand?

Where is your body in space?

_____
_____
_____
_____
_____
_____
_____
_____
_____
_____
_____
_____
_____
_____
_____
_____
_____
_____
_____
_____
_____
_____
_____

What do you see, smell, hear, feel, and taste?

What is your present level of comfort as you ask yourself, "What am I thinking and feeling RIGHT NOW?"

_____

_____

_____

_____

_____

_____

_____

_____

_____

_____

_____

_____

_____

_____

_____

_____

_____

_____

_____

_____

_____

_____

_____

_____

_____

Practice

Hold yourself Accountable. Incorporate Soul Work as a Way of Life.

With most things, practice helps us begin to ingrain new habits, beliefs, or attitudes. When you follow the order of these elements, in time, the sequence falls into place. The challenge is to practice. Once you get a taste of conscious choice, it's hard to go backwards.

What do you struggle with? Do you struggle with accountability?

_____

_____

_____

_____

_____

_____

_____

_____

_____

_____

_____

_____

_____

_____

_____

_____

Which elements of Soul Work are easy for you to write about? Why?

_____

_____

_____

_____

_____

_____

_____

_____

_____

_____

_____

_____

_____

_____

_____

_____

_____

_____

_____

_____

_____

_____

_____

Which elements of Soul Work are difficult for you to write about? Why?

Sacred Space

When you begin to **connect**, **trust** your **vulnerability**, and find the **courage** to have **compassion**, **self-care** creates the time and space to **reflect** and **remember**. As you **allow** what is arising to come to the surface, **acceptance** of what is **present** becomes the **practice** of feeling "at home" – whatever that means for you in your heart – your **sacred space**.

What, where, when, how, and with whom do you feel a sense of safety?

_____

_____

_____

_____

_____

_____

_____

_____

_____

_____

_____

_____

_____

_____

_____

_____

What do you find sacred?

The Importance of Knowing Thyself

After reading *Soul Warrior*, What have you learned about yourself?

_____

_____

_____

_____

_____

_____

_____

_____

_____

_____

_____

_____

_____

_____

_____

_____

_____

_____

_____

_____

_____

_____

_____

Reconnect and Rejoice

What brings you joy?

Offer

If you are interested in connecting with me as your guide, exploring what aspects of yourself feel out of alignment, and embarking on a journey towards who you truly are, please contact me. I offer each new client a free, 30-minute Clarity Call and you may reach me through my website. Know that I look forward to hearing from you.

www.angeladesalvo.net

What are your dreams?

_____

_____

_____

_____

_____

_____

_____

_____

_____

_____

_____

_____

_____

_____

_____

_____

What do you offer the world?

What is your purpose?

How can I best offer my services to you?

THE END

REFERENCES

Gibran, Kahlil. 1972. Beloved Prophet: The Love Letters of Kahlil Gibran and Mary Haskell and Her Private Journal. New York: Knopf.

Hillman, James. 2017. The Soul's Code: In Search of Character and Calling. New York: Ballantine Books.

O'Donohue, John. 2005. *Divine Beauty: The Invisible Embrace.* New York: Harper Perennial.

Riso, Don Richard & Russ Hudson. 1999. The Wisdom of the Enneagram: *The Complete Guide to Psychological and Spiritual Growth for the Nine Personality Types.* New York: Bantam Dell.

Rogers, Fred. *You Are Special: Neighborly Wit And Wisdom From Mister Rogers* https://www.goodreads.com/quotes/913279-as-human-beings-our-job-in-life-is-to-help Accessed 24 May 2022.

Suzuki, Shunryu. 2011. Zen Mind, Beginner's Mind: Informal Talks on Zen Meditation and Practice. Boulder, Colorado: Shambhala-Trade.